Wakefield Press

THWACK!

Ashley Mallett is a former Australian Test cricketer and a born storyteller. Over a long writing career, Ashley has written biographies on famous people, 14 children's books, historical sports books including *The Black Lords of Summer* and a detailed history of the Australian Aboriginal 1868 cricket tour of England, and much more.

Thwack! The glorious sound of summer is Ashley's 34th book.

By the same author

Autobiography
Rowdy
Spin Out

Biography
Clarrie Grimmett – The Bradman of Spin
TRUMPER – The Illustrated Biography
Chappelli Speaks Out
One of a Kind – The Doug Walters Story
Thommo Speaks Out
Nugget – Man of the Century
Scarlet: Clarrie Grimmett, Test cricketer
No Beating About the Bush
The Diggers' Doctor

Historical
The Black Lords of Summer
The Catch that Broke a Bank
Great Australian Test Cricket Stories
The Magic of Spin
Bradman's Band

General non-fiction
100 Cricket Tips
Eleven: The greatest eleven of the 20th century
The Boys from St Francis

Master Sportsman Series for children
Cricket: *Doug Walters*; *Dennis Lillee*; *Rodney Marsh*; *The Chappell Brothers*; *Allan Border*; *Geoff Lawson*; *Kim Hughes*; *Don Bradman*
Football: *Mark Williams*; *Tim Watson*; *Robert Flower*; *Wayne Johnston*
Soccer: *John Kosmina*
Tennis: *Evonne Cawley*

Thwack!

The glorious sound of summer

Ashley Mallett

Wakefield Press

Wakefield Press
16 Rose Street
Mile End
South Australia 5031
www.wakefieldpress.com.au

First published 2020

Copyright © Ashley Mallett, 2020

All rights reserved. This book is copyright. Apart from
any fair dealing for the purposes of private study, research,
criticism or review, as permitted under the Copyright Act,
no part may be reproduced without written permission.
Enquiries should be addressed to the publisher.

Cover designed by Stacey Zass
Edited by Julia Beaven, Wakefield Press
Typeset by Michael Deves, Wakefield Press

ISBN 978 1 74305 778 0

 A catalogue record for this book is available from the National Library of Australia

Wakefield Press thanks Coriole Vineyards for continued support

THWACK!

The sound of summer, a ball and a THWACK!
Willow meets leather, there's no turning back
to the cold and the gloom of the winter chill.
Bring on summer the THWACK! and the thrill.
Larwood to Bradman played out on the sward.
Off colour is Larwood now put to the sword.
A Don Bradman pull brings a six or a four
and Larwood the bowler is shown the door.
The slow man of class arrives at the wicket,
Bradman's eyes narrow as he looks at the picket.
The ball lands too short to complement its spin
Bradman's eyes light up, the willow must win.
The sound of summer, a ball and a THWACK!
Willow meets leather, there's no turning back.

Ashley Mallett

Contents

Preface		ix
1	Bumble and the pink box	1
2	Chappelli's softer side	4
3	Martin Crowe: he wore the black cap proudly	8
4	Freddo's day in the sun	10
5	Victor Trumper: the father of rugby league	14
6	The catch that broke the bank	18
7	Hazare's Adelaide magic	27
8	The Boy Bradman	31
9	Mike Denness: the first Scot to captain England	39
10	A Royal leg-break	42
11	Rocket Mann: boy wonder of leg-spin bowling	45
12	England in Australia 1907–08: a baggageman's inside story	50
13	That elusive image	55
14	'Please, Mr Stoddart'	58
15	Have two and that will do	60
16	CHO	63
17	The first 'Mankad' in Tests	68
18	Lillee the firebrand	72
19	The art of cricket	75
20	Viv Richards: Master Blaster	79
21	'Fiery Fred' Trueman	85

22	Tibby Cotter's last charge	90
23	Ian Michael Chappell: our best Test captain	92
24	Jonny's band of courage	115
25	The 12th Man: the full story	118
26	Charlie Puckett: Iron Man	128
27	Bodyline Adelaide	132
28	Belief	136
29	Bingo!	144
30	The haven Adelaide	148
31	The Oval: my spiritual home	158
32	Bradman versus Warne	161
33	Best little Test match ground in Australasia	168
34	'Rice bowls and Paddy fields'	172
35	Breaking the rhythm	179
36	Gubby Allen: the England bowler who defied Jardine	185
37	Erapalli Prasanna: spin wizard	189
38	Catalyst for change	193
39	Clarrie Grimmett	200
40	Greg Chappell made batting look all so easy	202
41	The Big Cat	206
Epilogue		209
Acknowledgements		213

Preface

'THWACK!' is indeed the sound of summer: that distinctive, exquisite sound made when a cricket bat meets headlong with a red-leather cricket ball.

This book explores the joy of cricket through stories of the enduring game that has fascinated young and old for hundreds of years. I have written many and varied tales for your enjoyment. The tales cover anecdotes of the game's greatest players including Bradman, Sobers, Lillee, Warne, Ian and Greg Chappell, Lloyd, Viv and Barry Richards, Bill O'Reilly, Clarrie Grimmett, Graeme Pollock, and a host of others, all integral members of the *Walking Wisden*. In addition there are stories to delight from the not-so-familiar names, tales from 'the outer', and some famous people including a delightful look at the life and times of that ex left-arm wrist spinner and globally acclaimed lyricist Tim Rice. The beauty of *THWACK!* is that even the 'time poor' can find a few moments to pick up the book and read just one or two stories. Each story stands alone: some are lengthy, others can be read in a few minutes. All tales are designed to inform and entertain.

This is a book for all cricket lovers. Enjoy.

Ashley Mallett, Adelaide, 2020

Chapter 1

Bumble and the pink box

David 'Bumble' Lloyd possesses a quizzical – almost comical – face, which immediately brings a smile to your face. Apologies to Rowan Atkinson – or maybe it is a compliment – for Bumble has that Mr Bean sort of face, has he not? The instant Bumble starts to speak you find yourself smiling. He's a delight to any listening audience be it radio, television or whenever he stands to speak at a dinner. The Lancashire and England batsman came to Australia with the team lead by Mike Denness. The England batsmen were pretty much cock-a-hoop; all of their top players were in good touch and they didn't believe the propaganda filtering down the line about Dennis Lillee and a man named Thomson. Lillee was returning from a crippling back injury and Jeff Thomson was thought to be a wayward slinger; quick, some said, but erratic and he didn't swing the ball at all. All was revealed in the first Test at the Gabba, with Lillee returning to Test match cricket fitter, meaner and with better rhythm than ever. Jeff Thomson? Well, well. Thommo simply blew them away with speed never before seen at the Gabba.

The great England fast man Frank 'Typhoon' Tyson bowled there in 1954–55 and West Indian speedster Wes Hall bowled with a pace like fire against Australia in 1960–61, and in subsequent outings for Queensland in Sheffield Shield, but they did not compare to the whirlwind the England side of November 1974 faced in that first Test. Thommo shattered stumps and England's collective batting heart with a blistering 6/46 in the England second innings. His sandshoe crusher (a searing yorker) which clean bowled Tony Greig was a ball to behold.

With openers John Edrich and Dennis Amiss nursing broken hands and David Lloyd returning to the fold after missing the Gabba Test with a finger break, the plight of the England batting was pretty much forgotten in view of the flood of publicity over the recall of England's ageless war-horse batting star, Colin Cowdrey. Talk of Santa Claus and *Dad's Army* emerged, but Cowdrey was keen to put on a good show. The second Test was played on the lightning-fast WACA Ground pitch in Perth. Australian captain Ian Chappell won the toss and had no hesitation in making England bat. Brian Luckhurst fell first up, cutting a ball from Max Walker to me in the gully. Then Cowdrey, weighed down by so many pads under his shirt that Lillee laughingly quipped 'Ah, England's latest knight, all ready for a joust', walked to the crease to join David Lloyd, who had found the combination of Lillee and Thomson to be the battle of his cricketing life. At lunch Lloyd was unconquered on 25, Cowdrey was not out 9. What a fight it had been. The crowd loved it and Rod Marsh, standing 40 metres back to take Thommo's blistering deliveries, would mutter under his breath, 'Jeez that hurt ... but I love it!' All the Australians close to the wicket could clearly hear the tremendous smack of the ball into Marsh's gloves and were of the same opinion: thank the Lord Thommo's playing for Australia. Drinks were taken an hour after lunch and the England score stood at a respectable 1/99. No gremlins, it seemed, in the pitch. Earlier Cowdrey had copped a barrage of searing deliveries from Thomson, four of which struck him on the shoulder and the chest. At the end of the over Cowdrey walked up the bowler's end and, as Thommo was taking his jumper from the umpire, Cowdrey extended his right hand and said, 'Colin Cowdrey, Jeff. Nice to meet you.' Then Cowdrey joined Bumble between overs and said: 'I say Bumble, this is all jolly good fun.'

'Fun? Fookin' fun? You've got to be joking. I can't believe it.'

Poor old Bumble, he had a look of horror on his face and much have thought the Kipper had lost his mind; it was a bit like a condemned man making friends with the hangman at the foot of the gallows. With England battling away under a cloudless sky and the score going along nicely Thommo floored Bumble with a brute of a ball that hit him fair and square in the nether region. Poor Bumble. He fell in a screaming heap. What we players who gathered around Lloyd as he writhed on the pitch didn't know was that the batsman was wearing one of those pink plastic abdominal protectors. Cricketers call this piece of equipment a box, and Bumble's pink box had split in two. Little wonder Bumble was screaming in pain for he had one testicle inside the split box and one testicle outside: one ball in, one ball out. Effectively he was experiencing an extremely painful pinching of the balls. It took Bumble quite some time before the game resumed and he was out for a brave 49, following a lifting Thommo delivery and nicking it to Greg Chappell at second slip.

Bumble played just nine Tests for England, scoring 552 runs at an average of 42.46. His highest score, of 214*, was against India. He played 407 matches, mostly for his beloved Lancashire, hitting 19,269 runs at 33.33. He umpired first-class cricket for some time and coached the England team but his enduring cricket role is as a commentator. Bumble is the epitome of fun.

Working for Sky TV and company some of his quips are fabulous. Here's a sample:

Ian Botham: 'Where were you last night?'

Bumble: 'An oyster bar. Apparently it puts lead in your pencil. I don't know about that. I think it only matters if you've got someone to write to.'

Once he was quizzed over a woman asking him if he could autograph her cleavage.

'She was a lovely lady. Quite ample. In fact Muttiah Muralitharan would have had plenty of room to sign his name.'

Bumble has written a number of hilarious books including his autobiography *Last in the Tin Bath* (Simon & Schuster, UK).

Cricketer, TV commentator, umpire, coach, journalist, author, stand-up comic, Bumble is one of the most natural funny men on this planet. What we need in this complicated, politically correct world of ours is a good old dollop of British humour Bumble style. And the one story Bumble loved to dine out on, in fact still does? Yes, you guessed it, he tells this story, albeit with a tear in his eye, the Perth Test match tale of Bumble and the pink box.

Chapter 2

Chappelli's softer side

Throughout his successful sporting career ex South Australian and Test captain Ian Chappell was universally known for his tough, sometimes abrasive, take-no-prisoners approach. Chappelli could sledge with the best of them, but at times it was very funny. In 1972 we played the Combined Universities at Oxford. Bob Massie was swinging the ball all over the place and their first drop, Dudley Owen-Thomas, had trouble getting a bat to any Massie delivery. After being rapped on the pads for the umpteenth time, Owen-Thomas got down on one knee to do up his bootlaces. It was the end of the over and he noticed the first slipper Chappelli walking past. Eyeballing our captain he said, 'I say, skipper ...' nodding towards his bootlaces: 'Piss off, pal,' Chappelli barked, 'I only do up the bootlaces for batsmen.'

At lunch Owen-Thomas, who had scored 52 before John Inverarity spun one past his forward defence to hit off-stump, sheepishly sidled up to Chappelli as he sat with team manager Ray Steele and to their amazement the Combined Universities number three said, 'I am so sorry for the way I batted out there this morning.'

This tough exterior is how everyone perceived Chappelli, yet there was – and is – a softer, compassionate side to him. When Chuck Fleetwood-Smith was down on his luck, penniless without a roof over his head, Chappelli came to his aid; he lifted Neil Hawke's spirit when Hawkeye was gravely ill in hospital; and he went to see my old mate Terry Jenner when TJ was suffering inner turmoil in prison.

CHAPPELLI'S SOFTER SIDE

Former Test batsman Ross Edwards has seen the softer side of Chappelli. They were playing for Australia against England at The Oval in the final Test of the 1975 Ashes series. Midway through the game Edwards received a telegram informing him of the death of a close friend and Chappelli, who had seen the telegram, quietly went to his teammate and said: 'Rosco, if you prefer not to go back on to the field next session, it's okay by me.'

I once asked Chappelli's mum, Jeanne, what had happened to Ian since he retired from cricket.

'Has he mellowed? Is there a soft side to Ian Chappell?'

'Boy, is there ever a soft side to him,' she laughed. 'There always has been, really.'

Chappelli rationalises his mellowing: 'I think every human being has a softer side,' he says. 'Why do you have wives and children and animals? You have them because you love them. I'm surprised that other people are surprised I have a softer side.'

In 2003 Chappelli toughness on the tennis court was challenged. He had won the Bayview Tennis Club championship doubles and was runner-up in singles.

'When I heard my opponent in singles was an 11-year-old kid, I spoke to my doubles partner Ken Grey and said, 'I'm not comfortable about playing against an 11-year-old. If I serve hard everyone will say I'm a prick.'

Grey laughed: 'If you don't serve hard he'll run you all over the court, Chappelli. You'd better be on top of your game or the kid will demolish you.' I served hard and 11-year-old Michael Clisby beat me in straight sets.'

Behind the microphone with the Nine commentary team, Chappelli is insightful in his comments and while he does not take a backward step, he mostly builds a balanced for-and-against argument. As a captain he was very much in the Mark Taylor mould: he created for his players an environment of trust, empowerment and enjoyment. He knew instinctively that if the workplace was a happy one his charges would give their all for the boss. The players in his Test teams revelled in the success of their teammates, an essential collective quality for successful sporting teams.

Much of Chappelli's early summer days were spent watching his father, Martin, play cricket. In winter he was the Glenelg Baseball Club batboy and this environment taught young Ian a few different words and phrases. Some of the words resonated and from that time on Chappelli tended to swear, more than occasionally.

One day, years later as he was presenting a *Nine Wide World of Sports* segment, there was a mix-up by the production crew and instead of the expected horse racing vision a US hot-rod spectacular appeared. Chappelli momentarily lost his cool, even uttering the magic word in front of the camera. Kerry Packer was watching the program at the very time of Chappelli's outburst. In the wake of an instant stand down, Packer summoned Chappelli to his office for a 'please explain'.

'Now, look here, son,' Packer said, 'I sacked Graham Kennedy for saying what you said on air, but he meant it. You didn't. You just couldn't help yourself. Don't do it again.'

Chappelli knew that he must heed Kerry Packer's thinly veiled warning. Another transgression like that one and his TV broadcasting career was kaput. Chappelli's wife Barbara-Ann told her husband that if he did not swear anywhere, at home, at the office or the pub, he would effectively solve the problem. When Garry Sobers heard about Chappelli's iron-willed resolution to avoid saying anything untoward, anywhere and at any time, he rang his friend.

'Hey, Chappelli, I hear you are not swearing anymore. That's interesting. Next time we meet up for a beer the conversation is going to be very one-sided and I suspect fairly dull because *I'll be doing all the talking*.'

***

Chappelli has taken up some good causes, including opposition to the Howard Government's handling of the *Tampa* crisis.

'I was yelling at the TV as the SAS boarded the *Tampa*. After a while Barbara-Ann said, 'Bad things happen when good people do nothing.' That made me think. Barb's words sort of got me off my backside. I guess I thought to my self, 'Yes, Barb's right. I just can't rail at the television set and do nothing. I am in a position where I have a public voice. Maybe I can do something here.'

Chappelli became a special representative for the United Nations High Commission for Refugees (UNHCR) and he put his name to a letter calling for donations to raise money for the Afghan refugees. Late in 2001 UNHCR's Naomi Steer rang him to say that some of the money raised was to be put towards redeveloping a playing field and to build a gymnasium in East Timor.

Later that year Chappelli received a call from journalist Mike Coward, who covered the 1972 Australian tour of England, asking him if he would like to become patron of A Just Australia, a group dedicated to just treatment of refugees.

'The aim is to achieve just and compassionate treatment of asylum seekers, consistent with the human rights standards that Australia has developed and endorsed,' he said.

In 2003 Chappelli was part of a delegation that met Immigration Minister Philip Ruddock calling for urgent changes to the treatment of asylum seekers being kept in long-term detention in Australia. The battle continues and knowing Chappelli there will be no turning back for him on this issue.

At the 2003 Allan Border Medal presentation, Chappelli gave a moving speech which heralded the induction of the 1868 Aboriginal cricket team to the Australian Cricket Hall of Fame.

Chappelli loves the game of cricket with a passion. He'll get with his mates and they chat over a beer or a good red. There's always good-natured banter and laughter. The stories sometimes get a bit embellished, but the blokes in his company love his passion, knowledge and extraordinary memory of a long-gone event.

He was a great captain, a mighty player. Chappelli was and remains a staunch fighter for the underdog. For those players who played under his leadership, Ian Michael Chappell is our captain for life.

Chapter 3

Martin Crowe:
he wore the black cap proudly

New Zealand cricketer Martin Crowe was a brilliant batsman. He had all the shots and, along with Bert Sutcliffe of old and Kane Williamson today, he ranks among the best ever New Zealand batsmen, hitting 5444 runs in 77 Tests at an average of 45. At the Basin Reserve, Wellington, in 1991, Crowe completed his highest Test score (299).

With Andrew Jones (186) the pair hit 467 runs for the third wicket, then the world record partnership for any wicket. The Crowe–Jones epic stand eclipsed the 451-run partnership by Australian legends Don Bradman and Bill Ponsford against England at The Oval in 1934. Sri Lanka's rotund skipper Arjuna Ranatunga grabbed the ball in sheer frustration that day in Wellington. An occasional slower-than-slow dibbly-dobber, Ranantunga shuffled in and bowled a wide 'nothing' ball. Crowe chased it wildly. He said later: 'The ball was delivered and I never saw it, it became a blur, and at the last second I thrust out my bat and the ball took the edge. It flew low and hard to Hashan Tillerkaratne and he held it inches from the ground. As the reality of what happened struck me, I began to storm off the field, striking a sign as I departed through the gates. I was in shock. At that moment I knew I had blown the very moment I had waited for my whole cricketing life.'

Back in the 1975–76 summer, the year South Australia won the Sheffield Shield under Ian Chappell, Dave Crowe brought his 14-year-old son Martin to Brisbane on the eve of our match with Queensland. Martin's brother

Jeff was then playing for SA and Jeff (known to all and sundry as 'Chopper') asked me if I would bowl to Martin in the nets.

The turf wickets were wet after recent rain so we had a workout on the artificial tracks at the Gabba. Despite Martin's youth, he was the talk of New Zealand. 'This kid will play Test cricket,' was on every Kiwis' lips. The ball bounced and spun and after hitting Martin on the side for the umpteenth time, he looked up and said with a gleam in his eye, 'You just wait until I get my black cap.'

We didn't have to wait long. Five years later he was playing for his country.

Martin loved playing at Adelaide Oval and he hit a Test century (137) there in 1987. But he also smacked the SA bowlers for a couple of big hundreds during the 1980s. He was a good mate of then SA captain David Hookes.

On 3 March 2016 Martin, affectionately called 'Hogan', died after a long battle with cancer. Hookes had died 12 years earlier, aged 49.

Right now he is probably enjoying a cold one with Hookesy upstairs.

Martin Crowe was a champion cricketer who wore the iconic black cap of New Zealand with pride. Crowe at the wicket had class, balance and timing. He was simply one of the best.

Chapter 4

Freddo's day in the sun

In a celestial blink the human dynamo that was West Indian opener Roy Fredericks set the heavens alight to enrich and delight the world of cricket. That day, 13 December 1975, was no ordinary day of Test cricket. Fredericks, or 'Freddo' as he was affectionately known, peppered the boundaries on the WACA Ground with a savagery and frequency that shocked Greg Chappell's Australian team. The sky was blue and the sun shone over Perth but the fours rained in a torrent, telling all and sundry that this was an innings for the ages: a knock that would have delighted the likes of Trumper, Bradman, Harvey and Gilchrist. Freddo lit up the firmament in a star-studded display and in just 145 balls he had scorched to 169 against an attack that included Dennis Lillee and Jeff Thomson: Lillee at his most fearsome and Thomson as his fastest. His hundred came in 71 balls. This was astonishing. Not a one-dayer, it was a Test match, for God's sake.

Freddo smashed the ball continuously, especially when he batted at the members' end, where he hit with the strong south-easterly which blew like a mini-cyclone. The dynamic Windies left-hander seemed to hit out more fiercely, perhaps knowing that an uppish Fredericks slash through backward point and travelling with the velocity of a tracer bullet was nigh on impossible to catch. There was Lillee hurling down his thunderbolts and Thomson bowling like the wind and Freddo cutting and pulling like a man possessed. There was many a time when Freddo cut at lifting deliveries and at the precise instant he struck the ball both of his feet were well clear of the ground. In effect, Freddo was leaping to the task of belting hell out of the Aussies.

The Fremantle Doctor added to our woes, the wind reaching 50 kph. Add that to the speed of Freddo's tracer bullet-like strokes.

My own experience was, to my mind, very much worse than the drubbing we received in the field from the bat of Roy Fredericks. The day before the Test I went straight from the WACA to visit a dentist. A week or so earlier, during the Brisbane Test match at the Gabba, I had occasion to visit a dentist, who drilled for all his worth at one of my back teeth, then filled it. All was, I thought, tickety-boo.

However, the pain in the tooth, the very one the Brisbane dentist had filled, was so intense I turned up at the Perth dentist, who said matter-of-factly: 'Do you want the good news or the bad news first up?'

He explained that the said tooth had to be extracted straight away. Then he announced: 'The tooth has to come out, but I am afraid an abscess has developed under the filling and no amount of anaesthetic will work. The tooth has to come out without it!'

The dentist then proceeded to extract the tooth, but he broke it off at the gumline, then continued unabated digging the root out with some sort of implement that resembled a torturous-looking hook from the Middle Ages.

Next day dawned bright and sunny. I bowled from the members' end and should have had Clive Lloyd out for a duck when he tried to launch me into Gloucester Park, the well-known totting track outside the ground, but succeeded only in skying the ball. There was Dennis Lillee under the ball. Fot's safe hands would do the job, I thought. (Lillee had been given the name 'Fot' early in his career. His WA captain, England spin bowling great Tony Lock, annoyed with the manner the young Lillee was bowling, admonished Lillee with the words, 'Dennis, you are bowling like a Fucking Old Tart.' Teammate John Inverarity cleverly took the first letter of each word and the nickname stuck.) But no, the wind took hold and Fot misjudged the catch. Lloyd, the Big Cat, went on to score 149. Alvin Kallicharran might also have left for a duck, but while beating him in flight, Rodney Marsh missed the stumping chance and Alvin scored 50-odd. On that day of no justice for me, I bowled 26 overs for a return of 0/103.

Sometimes it is not your day either on or off the cricket field.

Happily for the game, Freddo's innings was sublime. Those who played in the match and those who watched his mastery still talk of his remarkable innings: Freddo's Day in the Sun.

I was fielding in the gully and nothing came anywhere near me yet anything slightly within reach Freddo was cutting, the ball soaring over my head and to my left, around point, like a man in jungle combat delivering fatal blows with his flashing cutlass.

We batted first, our innings ending early on the second day for 329, Ian Chappell playing a grand innings of 156 against the Windies pace attack led by Andy Roberts and Michael Holding. The West Indians had 90 minutes to bat before lunch. Freddo hit Lillee's second ball for six, with a hook. This was some statement of intention. A few months earlier at Lord's in the first World Cup final ever played, Freddo hooked Lillee's first ball for six, then trod on his stumps. This time he decided to settle in for ... one ball.

At lunch the Windies had hit 130 for the loss of Bernard Julian's wicket. Just 14 8-ball overs had been completed: most time lost retrieving the ball from the stands and where it had rested miles beyond the eastern rope. The Windies' 200 came in just 22 overs and Freddo was out for 169 (caught by Greg Chappell at second slip off Lillee) with the score at 277. In the wake of Freddo's onslaught I forgave myself for thinking that the cricket gods had conspired against the Australian cricket team, both in a collective and individual sense.

But all that was forgotten in the wake of Freddo's amazing innings. I had three mates who conceded more than 100 runs: Lillee got 2/123 off 20 overs; Thomson 3/128 off 17; Gilmour 103 off 14 and Walker was let off lightly: 2/99 off 17. It was a thrashing of the highest order. Lindsay Hassett said on the ABC that Frederick's 169 was the 'greatest innings I've seen in Australia'.

Some accolade given Hassett played alongside Bradman from 1938 through to 1948 and had seen many amazing innings from Bradman and others. During World Series Cricket Freddo, a man edging towards 36 who seemed affronted by any suggestion to don a protective helmet, was clocked on the head by Graham, McKenzie and one other, yet he simply shook his head and batted on. Some of the Aussies dubbed him 'cement head'. Someone suggested Freddo called everyone 'old chap', although that wasn't my experience.

Whenever you bumped into the little bloke, he just seemed to mumble a greeting then his face lit up like a Christmas tree; like his batting that day at the WACA Ground in December 1975: the day all the stars in the firmament got together with the human dynamo Roy Fredericks to give the world of cricket an unmatched heavenly delight.

Chapter 5

Victor Trumper: the father of rugby league

Rugby league supporters can thank Victor Trumper, the greatest batsman of cricket's Golden Age, for the creation of the sport in Australia. Even when Trumper was the batting hero of Test cricket, he played rugby as fullback for South Sydney. And he wasn't afraid to throw himself into the fray, twice suffering a broken collarbone, which cost him a number of vital Sheffield Shield matches for NSW. Trumper had a problem with his double-jointed right big toe; every time he kicked a ball he had to take off his boot and put his toe back in place. He also knew that playing amateur sport could be a costly business. Concerned that rugby union had no practical insurance scheme to cover a player when he was injured led Trumper and two business associates to form a breakaway code they called rugby league. A rugby union player – Alec Burdon – was injured with his club, Sydney, during a northern rivers trip in 1907. Nursing a broken arm, Burdon lost a great deal of working time through his injury. Burdon received not a penny's compensation from the rugby union establishment. While Trumper was universally loved as a great cricketer and a man of humility and compassion, he was ever swift to act against or speak out against injustice. Trumper was among three men who considered Burdon's treatment from the NSW Rugby Union as at the very least a 'very poor show'.

The trio – Trumper, James Giltinan and Peter Moir – decided to act. They met at Trumper's Market Street store at a time when rugby union was enjoying peak popularity. The New Zealand 'All Blacks' v NSW match at the SCG in 1907 attracted a gate of 51,000 fans. At that time A.H. Baskerville was planning to take a New Zealand professional team to England. Among the party was George Smith who cabled Peter Moir asking whether a match could be organised in Sydney before the team departed for the UK. Moir discussed the idea with others and another meeting was set up at Trumper's shop. The meeting comprised Trumper, Giltinan, Alec Burdon and Harry Hoyle. Terms were sought for three matches in Sydney. Baskerville and team manager H.J. Palmer accepted three dates in August. Giltinan guaranteed £500 for the three matches and advised that they would be played on the Agricultural Ground, part of an area of land proclaimed by Governor Macquarie in 1811 and which later became known as the Showground, venue for the Agricultural Society's Royal Easter Show. Trumper and Giltinan, who were then business partners, outfitted the team and provided all necessary equipment.

The first match between NSW and the rebel New Zealand rugby league teams attracted a sell-out crowd of 20,000 people. The NSW Rugby League was formed on 12 August 1907 and Trumper was its first honorary treasurer. During his time as treasurer Trumper was accused of mismanagement of league funds. However, there was never any evidence of Trumper having used league money for his own gain. In 1908 Trumper was one of the auditors for the NSW Referees' Association – surely a post not likely to have been bestowed upon a man who was not trusted implicitly by the code's power brokers.

Trumper was also instrumental in getting the South Sydney Rabbitohs up and running. South's most famous player was undoubtedly the 'little master' Clive Churchill and its most famous modern benefactor, actor Russell Crowe.

The inextricable link between cricket and rugby league may well be the unique double-V on the Kangaroos' jumper – a design that may well have been a deliberate Trumper-take on the V-style neck piping on Australian sweaters.

It is amazing that two prominent cricketers from Australia's colonial cricketing days – Victor Trumper and Tom Wills – had such an impact on different major sports. Wills brought Australian Rules Football Down Under. After attending Rugby School in England in the 1850s, Wills returned to Australia and, with help from his cousin Henry Harrison, he developed a crude form of Australian Rules Football to help cricketers 'keep fit during the winter'. On 31 July 1858, the first recorded match was played on Richmond Paddock between Melbourne Grammar School and Scotch College. Only illness and, sadly, his premature death at the age of 37 in 1915 prevented Trumper from continuing an administrative role in rugby league, or, in fact, becoming involved in the union movement or indeed state or federal politics, given that he was a champion of the downtrodden and underpaid.

As a cricketer Trumper's last great stand was at the Sydney Cricket Ground just over 100 years ago. Late in the summer of 1913 the people came in their droves to the Sydney Cricket Ground to salute their hero. Victor Trumper, the greatest batsman in cricket's Golden Age, didn't let them down. On the third day of Trumper's benefit match between NSW and the Rest of Australia he hit a majestic 126 not out. Don Bradman was then seven years of age, living with his mother and father in Bowral, and it was a year before the calamitous events of 28 June 1914 when the assassination of Archduke Franz Ferdinand of Austria sparked the outbreak of World War I. But from 7–11 February 1913 cricket lovers saw the magic of Trumper's batting in his last brilliant display on the coveted SCG turf, forever his field of dreams.

Trumper captained NSW against a Rest of Australia team led by Clem Hill and featuring Warwick Armstrong, Vernon Ransford, Edgar Mayne, Jack Ryder, Johnnie Moyes, Bill Whitty, Tom Matthews, Jack Crawford and Les Cody. Among Trumper's teammates were Charles Kelleway, Charlie Macartney, Warren Bardsley, Herbert Hordern, Herbie Collins and Hanson Carter. Carter, a one-time business partner of Trumper's and by profession an undertaker, was also a Paddington teammate and used to take his horse-drawn hearse to club matches. Carter was the first Test wicketkeeper to crouch down behind the stumps while the bowler was approaching the wicket.

In his book, *A Century of Cricketers* (Angus & Robertson, Sydney, 1950) Johnnie Moyes, who played in Trumper's benefit match, said this of the great batsman: 'He expressed the view that we had treated him rather generously in the matter of an LBW decision and he proceeded to 'give us a chance'. I saw him with a flick of the wrists lift a fast rising ball from Jack Crawford on to the cycle track, which in those days encircled the ground. I saw him vary it by cutting a similar ball for four. In the same over, Trumper jammed down on a fastish yorker and turned it away past square leg to the fence. This is not imagination, for I was fielding in the slips and I saw it and marvelled. One of the choicest memories of my life is that I was privileged to see Victor at close quarters, to watch his wizardry.'

Trumper received a total of £2950.13.3 for his benefit match, a then record for any Australian Test player: a record, that is, until the 1948–49 season when Don Bradman's benefit game in Melbourne fetched a tidy £9432.

Former NSW premier and governor-general, Sir William McKell, was aged 92 when we spoke over the telephone in early 1984. He told me how as a 10-year-old boy he would spend his every summer Saturday morning, when Victor Trumper was playing for Paddington, travelling by tram to watch his hero play. At the age of 21 McKell watched the Trumper benefit match and he saw every run of his hero's brilliant 126. In 1984, Sir William, frail in body but fit in spirit, sent me his personal memento – a splendid photograph of Trumper with facsimile autographs of all those who played in the match. Trumper was revered by all who knew him and one man, Neville Cardus, perhaps the nearest to Shakespeare any cricket writer could hope to attain, has the last word:

> As I look back on my boyhood and try and think of all the formative influences that made me a man of some awareness to the things of the imagination, I realise the power of three strangely diverse forces, each evocative of colour and romance – the music of Wagner's, Turner's canvas *The Fighting Temeraire* and Victor Trumper. I do not hesitate at this high prime of my life to write the name Victor Trumper along with those two immortals of a higher plane of artistic activity.

Chapter 6

The catch that broke the bank

The great cricketer, William Gilbert Grace, opened the curtain of his coach and was enveloped in choking dust. It was March 1874 and the new European colony of South Australia was bereft of infrastructure. If there was a Minister for Roads, he deserved a damned good thrashing.

W.G. Grace led the visiting England cricket team. His men had travelled overnight to make the 100-mile journey from the little country town of Kadina to keep their appointment in Adelaide. They were in good hands for the coach was driven by John Hill, later to become the father of the great left-hander, Clem Hill. John was a good horseman and a capable batsman who later scored the first century for South Australia. Coachman Hill had to call upon all his skill at the reins as the way was treacherous and bumpy and the visitors were parched and near exhaustion by the time they reached the 'big smoke'.

Grace had negotiated with the South Australian Cricket Association treasurer, Alexander Crooks, to accept £110 to play the three-day match, plus half the gate money. Before the deal was struck there was consternation about arrangements. Grace's team had demanded £800 from the South Australian Cricket Association (SACA) to agree to play a match at the Adelaide Oval.

The SACA was incensed when it learnt that the little town of Kadina, on Yorke Peninsula, had cornered all South Australian rights for the England matches of the 1873–74 season. While SACA officials seethed, the England team experienced a rough sea passage from Melbourne to Port Adelaide. On behalf of the team, Grace demanded that the England party travel to Kadina by coach. W.G. got his way.

He found to his dismay that the cricket ground at Kadina was a patch of burnt earth covered with small pebbles. Legend has it that Grace's team batted first and WG faced the first ball from a big lump of a country lad who tore in like a runaway train and delivered a ball of astounding pace which beat W.G.'s defensive push and uprooted his middle stump.

W.G. calmly lent over, picked up the stump and banged it back into place with the handle of the bat, then replaced the bails and said with a cheery squeak: 'Well then, that's got the trial ball over. Bowl up, son ...'

This was the first major tour by an England cricket team since the teams in 1861–62 and 1863–64, led respectively by H.H. Stephenson and George Parr, and these teams played almost exclusively in the eastern states. Persuading W.G. to tour 'Down Under' was a mini-miracle in itself. When the Melbourne Cricket Club's (MCC) then administrative head for cricket in Australia approached him to lead an England team on a tour of Australia, W.G. demanded a fee of £1500, exclusive of all expenses. The MCC shelved the idea, but to bring an England team to Australian without the redoubtable W.G. Grace seemed absurd. So it was in 1872 the Melbourne, East Melbourne and South Melbourne cricket clubs formed a management committee, who came to terms with W.G.

It was agreed that the amateur W.G. Grace was to receive £1500, plus all expenses, and each of his teammates, all professionals, would get £170, plus expenses. In H.H. Stephenson's 1861–62 party, the professionals had each received £250, exclusive of 'incidental extras'.

After a brilliant century in 58 minutes at Ballarat, W.G. was in good touch, but he was hardly required in Kadina where the locals managed only 42 in their first innings and 13 in the second. While the deal struck with SACA seemed a long way short of the £800 W.G. wanted, he negotiated the £110, plus half the gate money for the Adelaide game. The three-day match drew 15,000 spectators, an extraordinary attendance, given the entire population of Adelaide at that time was fewer than 200,000. Due to the deplorable conditions of the Kadina–Adelaide road, W.G.'s men arrived late and the match did not get underway until 3.30 pm.

Despite the late start, this day, Thursday 26 March 1874, was to mark the beginning of international cricket for South Australia. European settlement in Adelaide was barely into its 38th year and it was still three years before the first Test match was played at the MCG.

W.G. won the toss and invited civil servant Alex Lumley's locals to bat first. Alexander Crooks, who featured more prominently later in the game, opened the batting with Thomas Cole. Both fell for inglorious ducks, although if ever there was an audacious duck in the game of cricket it was achieved by Crooks. He threw caution to the wind and jumped down the pitch to the wiles of the slow-medium left-hander James Lillywhite, only to miss the ball completely and be stumped by John Bush.

Lillywhite was a fair bowler. He had taken 10/29 in a South versus North match at Canterbury in 1872. In addition, Lillywhite had taken 8/29 in his first-class debut for Sussex against the Marylebone Cricket Club at Lord's in 1862. His final first-class fixture was for Lord Sheffield's Eleven at Lord's in 1885. He was a nephew of Frederick Lillywhite, who had set the bar by taking all 10 wickets in an innings for Players versus Gentlemen at Lord's in 1837.

James Lillywhite led England in the first two Test matches. Dismissing the SACA treasurer Alexander Crooks might not have been the most thrilling cricket moment of Lillywhite's career, but the Adelaide Oval crowd saw in Crooks a man prepared to take a risk. The colony would later learn the extent to which Crooks was prepared to take risks. Crooks' duck was a failure among many, for the side managed a paltry 63, and then stumps were taken. The Englishmen looked forward to some refreshment and the prospect of batting straight away on the Friday. Only two England bowlers had a turn at the crease: James Southerton who took 13/24 and Lillywhite, 8/38.

Friday morning (27 March 1874) dawned grey and ominously overcast. W.G. looked down onto the street from his Hotel York window, noting the energy and bustle of a town eager to get to the Adelaide Oval. The *South Australian Register* reported that day, 'the Association in their efforts to make the affair a success, were ably supported by the public who consented to something like a cessation of business on Friday afternoon, although to do so on the day preceding the departure of the English mail must have caused much inconvenience. A half-holiday was made at the Government Offices, and the banks (with the exception of the Bank of Australasia) closed at noon, as did many of the wholesale Establishment and several of the retail businesses'.

Men in top hats, ladies in their finery, all armed with umbrellas, men wheeling trolleys, hansom cabs in waiting and urchins playing marbles and hopscotch within easy eye of the fat policeman, who wandered across the street to join John Bush in a pipe, adorned the main street of the colony. Grace mumbled and prepared to breakfast. The scene in the street made perfectly good sense to him, for the people of Adelaide were keen to see him bat.

A crowd of 5000 spectators flocked to the ground to watch the noon start to the day's play. A further 2000 non-paying spectators stood on Montefiore Hill looking down on the new ground, the spacious Adelaide Oval, created by an Act of Parliament in 1871.

The *South Australian Register* reported on 28 March 1874:

> In the England innings, Greenwood (15), Gilbert (12) and Humphreys (2) fell before W.G. Grace walked to the crease amid tumultuous applause. Grace was then a strong, athletic type, sporting a luxuriant beard. He bristled with muscles and he could have doubled for Ned Kelly. Grace wore the harlequin cap of the Marylebone Cricket Club. The strength and power of young W.G. Grace might be best illustrated by the athletic prowess he demonstrated so grandly in 1868.

In May of that year W.G., then aged 20, ventured down to The Oval in Kennington, London, to watch the Australian Aboriginal cricketers play Surrey. At the end of the first day's play there were a variety of spear and boomerang throwing demonstrations and later the long throw.

W.G. took up the challenge, throwing a cricket ball against the Aboriginal and Surrey players. He won the long throw with the wind with a throw of 109 yards and then proceeded to toss the ball 105 yards into the wind.

Six years later W.G. was in Adelaide playing for England against the Colonials. He yearned for a good score.

The *South Australian Register* commented:

Mr W.G. Grace next went in, and as he advanced to the wicket to take his maiden hit on the Oval, he was loudly cheered from all parts of the field ... The Champion made a hit for a brace, and then Cole delivered a maiden to Oscroft. The next over witnessed the downfall of the Champion. The second ball was hit by Mr Grace and it would have dropped outside the chain but a magnificent catch was made by Crooks and the mighty cheer which arose showed how greatly this splendid piece of fielding was appreciated. Mr Grace evidently seemed astonished at being taken in that style.

W.G. Grace was out; caught Crooks bowled Alex Lumley.

All the South Australia players rushed to embrace their new-found hero, Alexander Crooks, as the enraged W.G. Grace slumped off the field. From that moment Crooks, who took the catch to defeat the Champion, was Adelaide's best. Choked with emotion, men in suits and top hats grasped Crooks' hand. Suddenly the SACA treasurer was some sort of demi-god, to be admired, glorified. Ladies flirted with him and there were numerous offers for Crooks at day's end to partake in the demon drink. Crooks did not bat in South Australia's second innings, the scorebook listing him as 'absent ill'.

How could the wiseacres of the colony have known that Alexander Crooks' catch would be a catch that broke the Commercial Bank of South Australia?

England scored 108 and 3/38 to convincingly beat the colonials by seven wickets. The locals, batting a second time, scored 82, Grace taking 8/40 and Farrington Boult 8/30, the remaining four batsmen run out by some rather sharp England fielding.

Despite the loss, it was Crooks' catch that won widespread admiration. Crooks' fame as the man who 'caught the Champion' won him unqualified entrée to the well-to-do of Adelaide. He rubbed shoulders with noted parliamentarian and businessman Sir Henry Ayers and businessman, lawyer and politician Charles Kingston. In 1879 Crooks was employed as an accountant with the newly established Commercial Bank of South Australia. Within a year he was installed as manager.

Crooks was born on 23 September 1847 in Leith, Midlothian, Scotland. He was the youngest of seven children to William Crooks and his wife, Ann (nee Thompson). The family sailed in the *Colooney* and reached Port Adelaide on 7 December 1852.

In the 1860s Alexander Crooks was employed as a bank clerk in Angaston, a predominantly English settlement in the heart of the Barossa Valley. It was then a fledgling wine-growing district, largely populated by German immigrants who had fled their homeland in the wake of religious persecution. On 18 September 1873, Crooks married Emily Birks at the Wesleyan church in Kent Town.

Under Crooks' management, the Commercial Bank of South Australia grew rapidly. From 1879 to 1886 its balance sheet increased from £221,130 to £1,909,537, and it had 26 branches in South Australia, plus a branch at Palmerston in Darwin. There were also offices in Melbourne, Perth and London. Alexander Crooks could certainly catch a cricket ball, but he was no financier. The bank's directors, however, saw in Crooks a man who would have his eye on the ball. Crooks succeeded the chief manager in the Commercial Bank of South Australia who had loaned £30,000 to someone who nicked off with the loot. The bank's board of directors ruled that directors could obtain limited advances. A director was permitted to travel to Victoria to buy a sheep station. He had limited funds, but was blessed with entrepreneurial flair. The director jumped at the opportunity to buy three 'bargains' and he put the bank in for £50,000.

Crooks did not bat an eye. He had been given the task of seeing that the loans made were properly monitored and could be repaid. He was not, however, inelastic and unimaginable. He was always prepared to look after a good friend. Despite their displeasure at the turn of events the bank's other directors relented and agreed to an advance of £22,000 to help the sheep stations along. By 1885, three years after the original deal, the Commercial Bank of South Australia had invested £132,000 in the three properties, which were worth only £60,000. On the surface Alexander Crooks' problem, up until 1885, was that he had been too lenient.

Crooks was still SACA treasurer when South Australia played its first

Inter-Colonial match, against Victoria in 1875. South Australia hosted James Lillywhite's Englishmen in 1877 and it was in 1878 that the coachman, John Hill, hit the first century on Adelaide Oval. Crooks presided over South Australia's first Test match, which began on 2 December 1884. On that first day an advertisement appeared on the front page of the *South Australian Register*:

> To show the great importance of this grand international contest ...
>
> > One hundred and seventy-three business houses will close at noon.
> > Government half-holiday ...
> > Bank half-holiday ...
> > In fact there will be no business done during the Great Match ...
> > Excursion trains for a week ...
> > Members are informed that Smoking will not be allowed in the Pavilion.
> > For the convenience of Smokers two large marquees have been erected.

A first day crowd of 7000 was promising but SACA suffered a huge financial loss. SACA secretary John Creswell persuaded Australia and England to play the Test for a guaranteed £450 each side. Patrons were asked to pay 2/- to enter Adelaide Oval and a further 2/- for their vehicle. An additional 2/- was to be paid for each of the occupants aboard the carriage. Unfortunately, the cost of admission, plus a hot north wind and accompanying dust, contributed to a lack of spectators and a loss of revenue.

England won the match by eight wickets. For the Australians, Percy McDonnell scored 124 in the first innings of 243. Local hero George Giffen was bowled by Bates for 4. He performed better in the second innings, scoring 47. A medium pacer with a penchant to cut the ball into the right-hander, Giffen opened the Australian attack taking 2/80 in the first innings and 0/19 in England's second innings.

It was soon after Adelaide Oval's first Test match that Alexander Crooks' world began to totter. Crooks was lending out money hand over fist, as unsecured loans to associates and mates. He loaned a collective £185,000 to various associates about Adelaide without authorisation from the bank's board of directors, who had no idea about Crooks' activities. No one bothered to check the bank's books. Crooks had his fellow directors bluffed.

Every six months directors received a fat dividend. They thought Crooks was doing a magnificent job.

They were unaware that he had delved into the bank vaults to provide their dividends. In fact, Crooks was a whiz at fixing the books. Crooks had become so cunning about tickling the till that it was nothing for him to steal £1000 from the teller's cash box and leave in its place a chit written on a piece of brown paper. One of these hand-written chits on a scrap of paper was for £1889 for the South Australian Cricket Association. Crooks' habits were catching, for soon his accountant, Mr Wilson, began issuing chits for cash he was pocketing.

On 24 February 1886 the Adelaide business community was shocked to its core when news broke that the Commercial Bank of South Australia had been suspended from trading. Three days later Crooks was arrested and charged with fraud. The collapse of the bank caused recrimination against its directors and managers. At a meeting in the Adelaide Town Hall there was a call to lynch Crooks. Charged with embezzling £5000, Crooks faced court. He was defended by Charles Kingston in the trial which began on 6 April 1886.

Crooks pleaded guilty and was sentenced to eight years' hard labour at the Stockade, Yatala. The judge said Crooks 'probably misappropriated between £20,000 and £30,000 and without the bank's approval had advanced customers to the extent of £278,000'.

The bank went into liquidation four years after Crooks had been appointed chief manager. Insolvency was a fate the SACA avoided through astute management and a secret loan from the brewer and parliamentarian Sir Edwin Smith. Crooks had been the SACA treasurer from 1874 to 1885. In October 1885 Crooks was appointed SACA chairman. He resigned at the monthly association meeting in December 1885, two months before he was engulfed by the scandal.

The bank's liquidators eventually paid shareholders 3/- in the pound. Crooks' accountant Mr Wilson did not escape the clutches of the law. His fraudulent dealings landed him a six-year prison term.

A model prisoner, Crooks was placed in charge of the Yatala Stockade dispensary. He was granted early release in October 1889 and the following year he moved to Western Australia where he became manager of Gray & Sons, a mining company at Norseman. He returned to Adelaide in 1923 and retired to Brighton, a near-Adelaide beach suburb.

Crooks acknowledged his shortcomings and became involved in the community, including regular attendance at his local Anglican church. He died on 29 August 1943, three weeks before his 96th birthday, at Brighton and was buried at St Jude's Church of England cemetery. Pre-deceased by his wife in 1932, Crooks left a son and two daughters.

Alexander Crooks will be forever remembered as the man who caught the great cricketer W.G. Grace, reaching high to catch the ball one handed as it threatened to clear the chain which marked the boundary.

It was indeed the catch that broke the bank.

Chapter 7

Hazare's Adelaide magic

Like Tchaikovsky's immortal *1812 Overture*, Ray Lindwall's movement was all rhythm and grace, a crescendo before a delivery of sublime power. If you looked closely you caught a glimpse of the bulging muscle at the Lindwall shoulder and as he delivered the ball it was the finale to a wonderful co-ordinated attack of body and mind. But the great Indian batsman Vijay Hazare was more than up to the task, and he launched into a ball of fulsome length and caressed it with the wave of his magic blade, the ball screaming past Neil Harvey at cover with the velocity of a tracer bullet, before slamming into the boundary pickets. This majestic cover drive brought Hazare's historic second century of the Adelaide

Test match. The crowd rose as one and among them was Hazare's mentor, a little man in a suit and grey felt hat, his hands clasped in victory above his head where he stood in the press gallery near the players' change-room high in the George Giffen Stand. This little man was none other than Clarence Victor Grimmett, the 'Bradman of Spin', who, by an unbelievable selection oversight, was omitted from Don Bradman's 1938 Australian team to England.

But a decade later, in January 1948, Clarrie was at the Adelaide Oval to see his protégé Vijay Hazare hit two magnificent centuries in the Test match. Grimmett's last Test series was under the captaincy of Vic Richardson against South Africa in 1935-36, where he took 44 wickets in the series at an average of 14. But he never again played for Australia. He had his heart set on the 1938 touring team, but was not selected. In the wake of that disappointment, Grimmett was offered £2000, plus expenses, to sail to India and coach His Highness the Rajah of Jath. He gladly accepted the offer, for £2000 was a veritable fortune in 1938, and more than double the fee Don Bradman's tourists received for the England tour.

Apart from coaching the Rajah of Jath and his younger brother, Grimmett also took a young, enthusiastic all-rounder under his wing, the promising 23-year-old Vijay Samuel Hazare. The old leg-spinner always considered himself a pretty good batting coach.

Once he handed me his Jack Hobbs autographed bat and asked me to play a drive. Upon my saying I couldn't bat and wanted to learn about bowling, he replied: 'Ah, I taught a young man to play the back cut on the boat to England in 1930 ... and Don Bradman was a fast learner!' At training in India, Grimmett threw tennis balls from close range at Hazare and the Indian always maintained that the Australia's coaching and encouragement helped him tighten his defence and learn to execute his strokes efficiently. Months after Grimmett returned to Australian from India he received a letter (dated 22 February 1939) from Hazare and it read (in part):

> Of course I played on behalf of the central India XI in which, I am glad to inform you, I scored 138 not out and captured 6/57. Again quadrangular matches were played at Surat and I was invited to play on behalf of 'Rest'. I made 66 and took 5/45 and 3/18.

World War II hampered Hazare's progress and he didn't play his first Test until June 1946, against England at Lord's. England debutant Alec Bedser stormed through the Indians with 7/49 and 4/96; Hazare, batting at four, hit a modest double of 31 and 34. He took 2/100 off 34.4 overs in England's 428; his victims Bedser (30) and Bill Bowes (2).

Down Under the Indian all-rounder hardly troubled the scorers with the bat until the fourth Test of 1947–48 in Adelaide. It was a game of firsts: Neil Harvey, arguably Australia's best batsman since Don Bradman, debuted in this game; Ray Lindwall took a career best 7/38 in India's second innings;

Don Bradman hit 201, before Hazare clean bowled him; Lindsay Hassett was unconquered on 198; and Sid Barnes hit a solid 112.

But the match belonged to Vijay Hazare. After the Indian hit two majestic centuries – 116 and 145 – Bradman was moved to say: 'Hazare is the most graceful batsman it has been my pleasure to watch.' It was a terrific compliment for Hazare, for Bradman had seen first-hand the artistry and style of Alan Kippax, whose batting was said to have been close to the beauty and style of Victor Trumper; also the glorious England left-hander Frank Woolley, the brilliance of West Indian George Headley and many others between the wars and just after hostilities ended in 1945.

Grimmett blamed Bradman for influencing his fellow selectors to omit him from the 1938 Test, and how ironic that the man Bradman 'dropped' would become Vijay Hazare's mentor.

Hazare's wonderful double was against the quality bowling of Lindwall and Keith Miller, at least as good, perhaps the best of all the great Australian fast bowling partnerships – the others being Ted McDonald and Jack Gregory in 1921, and Dennis Lillee and Jeff Thomson in 1974–75. Along with Lindwall and Miller, Hazare had to negotiate the left-arm medium-fast stuff from Ernie Toshack, the off-spin of Ian Johnson and leg-breaks of Colin McCool. Hazare played grandly. He walked to the wicket with India a precarious 5/133 in the first innings and with Dattu Phadkar (123) the pair set about restoring order. They hit 188 for the sixth wicket, but Australia's first innings total of 674 saw the Indians follow on. In the second innings Hazare came to the wicket with India 4/99. He batted like a man possessed. Cruising to 50 with elegant strokes, Hazare played deft cuts and pulls and wristy shots off his toes which appeared to gain pace the further the ball travelled, not unlike the magic of VVS Laxman, when he's in peak touch.

Hazare's double in Adelaide gave him hero status back home and huge respect in Australia. After his epic 145, Grimmett invited Vijay to Dundula, his home in leafy Firle, a suburb some 10 km east of Adelaide Oval. They spoke animatedly of their time together in India and enjoyed much laughter. Then Clarrie stood at the dinner table, raised his glass and toasted his protégée: 'Vijay, a toast. You have made me a proud man today.'

Indian cricketers have perhaps a greater bond with cricket tradition than any other people of cricket-playing nations. Maybe it is because their ancient culture is steeped in rich history. There is a certain mystique about India that Clarrie loved.

The Indian people exude a gentleness that belies the national character; manners and gentleness in some quarters can be misconstrued as weakness. Clarrie Grimmett knew better.

Hazare was destined to play 239 first-class matches, in which he scored 18,784 runs at an average of 58.06 with 46 centuries and a top score of 316 not out for Maharashtra versus Baroda in 1939–40. In 30 Tests he hit 2192 runs at 47.65 with seven centuries. Against Yorkshire at Bramall Lane in 1946, Hazare scored an unconquered 244. Grimmett too liked playing against Yorkshire. In 1930 he took 10/37 against them.

Just before war broke out Hazare wrote to Grimmett:

> Let me note here that this little success of mine in the cricket sphere is entirely due to your valuable instructions which I will never forget, at least in this life. I will also be thankful to you if you will in future, as in the past, kindly help me by giving necessary instructions.

The Indian batting maestro played his final first-class match in 1966–67 for President's XI versus West Indies, but his greatest feat on the biggest stage was his majestic Test match double against Bradman's team on the Adelaide Oval in January 1948. He was one of the modern torchbearers for excellence in Indian Test batsmanship.

India's first 'great' batsman was Kumar Ranjitsinghi, who played for England at the turn of the 20th century and later, in 1907, became Mahataja Jam Sahib of Nawanagar. Hazare came much later and charmed the world, leading the way for Indian batting pride before the likes of Chandrakant Borde, the immaculate and brilliant player of pace bowling, Sunil Gavaskar, the moustachioed and disciplined Ajit Waderkar, and Gundappa Viswanath. Later came the exquisite strokeplay of Rahul Dravid, VVS Laxman, Sachin Tendulkar and Virat Kohli. In January 1948, Vijay Hazare made Adelaide the venue for history in the making.

Chapter 8

The Boy Bradman

Don Bradman scored 1000 first-class runs before the end of May 1930, a colossal feat first achieved by W.G. Grace in 1895. On that 1930 tour, Bradman, 21, took England by storm, scoring 974 Test runs at an average of 139.14.

In the wake of England's Ian Botham getting 149 not out to turn the Leeds Test in 1981, then Bob Willis (8/43) skittling our men for a paltry 111 to bring about a miracle win by 18 runs, Test captain Kim Hughes complained about the sideways movement in the Leeds wicket.

Headingly, Leeds, was Don Bradman's happiest of hunting grounds in England, where he scored 334 in 1930; 304 (1934); 103 and 16 (1938); 173 not out in 1948: 930 runs at an average of 232.5. Sir Donald wrote in a letter to me (dated 26 June 1985): 'Far too many people seem to think that batting becomes impossible when the ball is swinging or seaming off the pitch. It has always done that at Leeds – I always found it playable!'

Perhaps everything that could be written of the adult Don Bradman has been written and rewritten. But what of The Boy Bradman?

At Bowral Primary School, in the summer of 1915–16, The Boy Bradman built a reputation as a cricketer. When the bell tolled to end another school day, Don didn't dally to chat to others. He was in a desperate rush to get home. He ran helter-skelter through the small township of Bowral, turned into Shepherd Street, hurdled the white-picket fence, breezed through the front door and, tossing his schoolbag in the hall and grabbing his cricket bat, he yelled, 'C'mon, Mum, how about bowling me down a few?'

Emily Bradman smiled. She calmly discarded her apron, shifted the kettle on the stove and dutifully followed her son into the backyard. As Mrs Bradman wheeled down her own brand of left-arm deliveries, she could never have imagined that the small boy facing her at the other end of the back lawn would one day become the greatest batsman the world has known.

Born in Cootamundra on 27 August 1908, Don was the youngest of five children. His brother Victor was four years his senior and there were three sisters, Islet, Lilian and Elizabeth May. After spending the first two years of his life in Yeo Yeo, the Bradmans moved to Bowral where his father, George, a carpenter by trade, tried his hand at farming. As there were few boys of his age living nearby, Don pretty much was left to his own devices. More often than not he was forced to train alone and his isolation became the mother of a remarkable method in gaining batting practice. Using the round tankstand in the backyard, Don would take up his stance in front of the back door, the 'stumps'. Using a cricket stump as a bat, Don would throw a golf ball at the tank stand then attempt to hit the rebounding ball. If he missed the ball he was usually clean bowled as the back door presented a large target. The rebounding golf ball came back at him at lightning speed, helping him develop amazing reflexes. Don not only had to contend with the speed of the rebounding ball, but also the manner in which the ball reacted after hitting the uneven ground on its way toward him. Little did he realise that this form of practice would enable him to become a genius with the cricket bat.

He even developed a good method of recording the score. Don wrote the names of famous cricketers such as Charlie Macartney and Johnny Taylor (Australia), Jack Hobbs and Frank Woolley (England), on scraps of paper and kept a running score. The power of the stroke determined how many runs he gave himself for the shot. If he belted the ball hard it constituted a boundary. A stroke of slightly lesser power registered three runs, and so on. Games usually lasted two hours, each innings lasting half an hour. Whenever a left-hander batted (such as England's Frank Woolley), Don would take up his stance as a left-hander.

One day when his mother dropped a ball short to Don he swiftly went back and across and pulled the ball like a shot out of a gun. Mother and son watched in horror as the ball careered straight through the lounge-room window where Lilian was at the piano practising her scales. So ended both lessons.

Don was also fond of the piano and Lilian taught him well. Later in life he entertained teammates and tourists on board ship and in taverns during his four trips to England with the Australian team.

One of his own compositions, 'Every day is a rainbow day for me', was introduced during a performance of the pantomime *Beauty and the Beast* at the Grand Opera House in Sydney in February 1931. For a number of years Don was a choirboy at St Jude's Anglican Church in Bowral, where he regularly attended Sunday school. The Bradman family hosted Saturday night sing-a-longs at their Bowral home and they were always happily enjoyed by family and friends.

When Bradman was a boy, Bowral Primary School boasted little in the way of sporting facilities. Don walked to school and before lessons began, and during the 15-minute recess and the 45-minute lunch break, the boys played a crude form of cricket. Stumps were drawn on the bell post and the bat was hewn from the branch of a gum tree. The ball was a composite of cork and rubber and the pitch red dirt. The boys wore no pads or gloves and helmets were something the soldiers wore in the trenches of the Somme. The common playground separated the junior school from the high school. There was a 'gateway' between the two pitches and Don would often stand there, longing to try his hand against the seniors. His chance would come soon enough.

An above-average student, Don had a particular liking for mathematics, for which he won a gold medal. From early on young Bradman yearned to be one up on all the others, racing the master to find the answer to a maths problem before he had written it on the blackboard. Often he won the day, calling out the answer, much to the delight of his peers and the chagrin of the master. He could express himself well and became a capable writer and good public speaker. Don played rugby union football for the school and in age group races he was the school's 100 yards, 220 yards, quarter mile and half mile champion. He was also an excellent tennis player. At the age of 11, Don played in his first big cricket match.

He was still in primary school, but made the team comprised of mostly high school boys. They played a match at Glebe Oval (later renamed Bradman Oval). Don came in at the fall of the second wicket, facing a hat-trick. The first ball almost bowled him neck and crop, but he survived to hit 55 not out. Next season Don scored his maiden century – the first of 211 centuries he was to hit in all matches. This time he was representing Bowral Intermediate High School against old rivals, Mittagong. Don thrashed the Mittagong attack to the tune of 115 not out in a team total of 156.

Next day the headmaster, Mr A.J. Lee, called the school to assembly: 'I understand that there is a certain boy who yesterday scored a hundred in a match. That is all very well, but it is no excuse for having left the bat behind.'

Don's last match for the school was again against Mittagong. He hammered 72 not out and Bowral won. Some schools refused to play against Bowral if Bradman was in the team and Mittagong went as far as making a formal request to Bowral School to leave Bradman out of its team or they would forfeit the match.

At the age of 12, Don acted as team scorer for the Bowral Town cricket team, which played in the Berrima District competition. His father drove an old truck and Don sat on a wooden box in the back. George Bradman had been a good country bowler and handy batsman. As a youngster he won a gold medal for his efforts with the ball one summer and he wore the medal with pride on his watch chain. Inevitably one day a team member didn't turn up to the game, so Don got his chance against Moss Vale. He batted at the fall of the eighth wicket, scoring 37 not out.

The next week Don was promoted to open the batting. Again he was unbeaten, hitting an unconquered 29. Senior player Don Cupitt was so impressed with The Boy Bradman that he presented him with a full-sized cricket bat. It was Don's first real bat. The others he had owned had been fashioned from gum-tree branches. Don's father cut 7 cm off the bottom of the bat to help the boy better handle its weight.

In the summer of 1920–21 George Bradman treated Don to a day at the Sydney Cricket Ground to watch an Ashes Test match. They caught the steam train from Bowral to Central Station, then a tram to the ground, the journey in itself an adventure for Don. The youngster wore knickerbockers, a freshly pressed shirt, tie, waistcoat and cloth cap. His shoes shone like the new ball taken by the Australian fast bowling pair, Ted McDonald and Jack Gregory. Thanks to the fast men, England was dismissed for 204. Father and son sat near the fence at the Paddington End. Don was enthralled by the batting of Charlie Macartney, the dashing Australian No. 3, and his heart leapt when Macartney launched into a magnificent cover drive off the wily medium-pacer Percy Fender.

The history and tradition of the ground was as important to Don as the brilliance of the cricket. At the tea interval the Bradmans strolled about the famous SCG, revelling in the atmosphere. Don stopped near the players' entrance, the thrill of Macartney's enthralling batting to the fore in his mind as he said to his father, 'I shall never be satisfied until I play at this ground.'

Don Bradman left school at the age of 14, taking a job as a clerk in Percy Westbrook's real estate firm. Amazingly, at the age of 15 Don Bradman gave cricket away completely, concentrating on his other sporting love, tennis. However, he returned to the fold the next season and by the time he was 17 Don was a team regular and secretary of the Bowral Town cricket team. Late in the 1925–26 season, Bowral found itself pitted against Wingello. Rivalry? Far more than that, the Bowral–Wingello contests were tantamount to 'war'. Wingello boasted 19-year-old Bill O'Reilly, a big, cumbersome quickish spinner who was something of a 'warrior bowler'.

The much-awaited Bradman–O'Reilly clash was seen by many as local cricket's version of David and Goliath. The day arrived and O'Reilly smiled when he saw Bradman struggling in his over-sized pads to get to the crease, but he soon learnt not to take this youngster lightly. After three let-offs early in his innings, Bradman flayed the Wingello attack, O'Reilly included. At the end of the first day, Bradman was unconquered on 234.

Big Bill threw back his head and bellowed for justice. The match was played over two Saturdays so O'Reilly spent all week bowling at the family's unguarded gate, hell-bent upon revenge.

My poem tells the tale:

THWACK!

The Battle of Bowral

*The Battle of Bowral in '25
Saw Bradman the Boy come alive.
His first joust with Tiger, Goliath of Spin,
200 not out, Don Bradman must win.*

*At 30 a leg-break caught The Don's bat,
An edged chance to slip; a drop and a drat.
Young Don escaped the chance of the flight:
First slip, the skipper, was lighting his pipe!*

*A flurry of fours and sixes to boot,
O'Reilly at day's end a sorry young coot.
The Don stood supreme, the hint of a grin,
Bill's belly on fire, his head in a spin.*

*Don so fluent, so strong and so keen,
Tiger's red hair stood out from his spleen.
The cocky young bat from Bowral had done
More than enough to ensure they had won.*

*At two-thirty-four the Don left the field,
Raging O'Reilly refusing to yield.
All through the week Bill bowled at a gate,
Bradman the Boy made the Tiger irate.*

*O'Reilly the demon had n'er been caned,
Don hammered Big Red, he cannot be blamed.
For Spin King O'Reilly to fume and to scheme,
The Don bowled O'Reilly? – impossible dream!*

*Fuming O'Reilly bowled full steam ahead,
He dreamed of revenge as he tossed in his bed.
Seven days of pure hell, no fitting reward,
For Spin King O'Reilly put to the sword.*

Second day of the match yet to be played.
O'Reilly's revenge: no more to be flayed.
Townsfolk in droves arrived just in time
To see the young warriors: a battle sublime.

They saw O'Reilly bowl that first spinning ball,
Young Don tapped his bat, a wicket must fall.
Arms wheeling away in the hot noon sun,
O'Reilly moved in, his homework was done.

Don eyed with suspicion that O'Reilly first ball,
His footwork so keen, his score so tall.
The ball fairly buzzed, an ace and a trump,
It pitched leg perfect and hit the off-stump!

Bradman was soon playing for the St George Club in Sydney. At the age of 18 he was the A grade captain. He had found digs with the NSWCA leading administrator Frank Cash. One Friday Don called in to see Dr Mick Bardsley for a dental check. In a letter to well-known Adelaide surgeon Donald Beard (dated February 1986), Sir Donald wrote : 'The dentist said I had pyorrhoea and must lose one of my double back teeth. Always trusting my medical advisers I said okay. But before I left the chair he had removed six teeth, three on each side.'

Nursing a bruised and swollen face, young Don caught the bus home and lay on a sofa, a large bowl by his side. When Frank Cash's wife arrived home from shopping she found Don on his side. Alarmed at the sight of all the blood she rang the doctor, who advised Don not to play next day.

'I was captain and I didn't want to let the side down, so I played,' Sir Donald continued. Bradman sent the opposition in and St George bowled them out by 4.30 pm. Much to the annoyance of the big crowd Bradman didn't come in at the fall of the first wicket. He waited until the eighth wicket fell and then walked to the wicket. 'I was roundly booed by the spectators (the only time I can remember) who knew nothing of the drama being enacted behind the scenes.'

Don Bradman survived to fight on the following Saturday. This time he was fully fit. He scored 116 not out. St George won the match and Bradman wrote: 'I went from villain to hero.'

When Bradman the Boy became Bradman the Man he took international cricket by the scruff of the neck and dominated like no other batsman before or since.

Chapter 9

Mike Denness: the first Scot to captain England

The cricketing gods chose Mike Denness to become the first Scottish-born cricketer to captain the England Test team. Although Douglas Jardine, who presided over Bodyline, was born of Scottish parents he was actually born in India, so Denness was the first Scot to captain England. It was a wise choice for Denness was a man of purpose and resolve, a man with a happy disposition and a caring soul. I first heard of him when I played a season for Ayr Cricket Club in the Scottish Western Union in 1967.

There were three things for a budding young cricketer whom the club had employed as a professional-cum-groundsman: learn all about the poet Robert Burns, buy a kilt, and take care not to do anything to upset the Ayr Cricket Club's ground convenor Bill Denness, Mike's dad. Learning more about Burns was fine, after all there is the Burns' Cottage in Alloway, a Mike Denness on-drive from the club ground at Cambusdoon. And I settled for a Farquarson clan kilt after getting one on the strength of my mother's maiden name (West). But for all that I couldn't get one past Bill Denness, who like his son presented the broadest of straight bats to the most curly delivery. Bill Denness' bedroom overlooked the square at Cambusdoon.

When tending the ground I succeeded in getting what Bill wanted, a light and dark effect: you know, the sort we see at every Wimbledon Championship. Alas, I couldn't get the cuts with the grain and against the grain straight. My light and dark meandered all over the place and never did I get it right.

Bill Denness hired and fired staff so I might have been dismissed early that summer had it not been for Mike, who was then playing for Kent. I discovered later that Mike intervened, explaining to his dad that wickets taken by the young colonial and not grass cut was best for the Ayr Cricket Club. So I stayed and improved enough to get to play for Australia against Mike Denness when he captained England.

When I heard that Mike was to lead England's 1974–75 tour of Australia, I set about organising with an Adelaide car yard a sports car bearing the England colours for the exclusive use of Mike Denness whenever he was in Adelaide that summer. So I got a photo in a kilt on the Brig-O-Doon and Mike got the use of a stunning sports car in Adelaide a few summers later.

In the Test series Mike and his fellow batsmen copped a battering from Jeff Thomson, who was bowling faster than anyone I've seen before or since, and a rejuvenated Dennis Lillee, who returned to the Test arena after more than a year out with a near-crippling back injury.

The pair formed a fearsome attack and the England batting was put to the sword; so much so that captain Mike Denness dropped himself from the fourth Test, but he need not have bothered because England lost that game and with it the Ashes fell to Australia. Mike returned for the Adelaide fifth Test, scoring a gallant 51, then 14, but again the side lost. However, in the final Test of the series at the MCG, Denness hit a magnificent 188 and England scored a massive 529 paving the way for the visitors to win by an innings. Then came the first Test against Australia at Edgbaston in 1975. Denness put us in after winning the toss and we scored a creditable 359. Then it rained, big time. In those days only the ends were covered and the main part of the pitch was laid bare to the elements. On that sodden track, Australia won easily by an innings and Denness was blamed.

The last address I had of Mike's was *Hanging Tree Lane*, near Hutton in Sussex. It was as if Denness had been accused of high treason for putting Australia in after winning the toss. Metaphorically the man was hanged, drawn and quartered for putting us in. In the wake of that loss Denness was sacked and he never again played Test cricket for England.

MIKE DENNESS: THE FIRST SCOT TO CAPTAIN ENGLAND

Thankfully he continued to play county cricket and we played alongside one another in the 1976 International Wanderers tour of South Africa. His former Kent teammate John Shepherd also toured with us and there was pandemonium one night in Durban when Shep was told to leave a licensed club on the pretext of not wearing a tie. Mike was one of the leaders to show the way. We didn't condescend to question the order, we left the premises en-masse, for we all knew the racist motive behind it: after all, here we were trying to bring cricket to all of the people in a South Africa which was being hamstrung by apartheid. Denness did well in a side, managed by Richie Benaud, which included the Chappell brothers Ian and Greg, Glenn Turner, John Morrison, Martin Kent, Bob Taylor, Derek Underwood and yours truly. He hit 81 and 35 in our win against a South African XI in Cape Town and fielded as enthusiastically and as well at cover point as he had ever done.

Denness also undertook some managerial work during the World Series years in Australia and while he loved the traditional game, he also wanted to further the development of a better deal for professional cricketers worldwide.

Mike continued to turn out for Essex until 1980. In all he played 501 first-class matches for Kent and England and with the International Wanderers in South Africa. After a long battle with cancer, Mike died on April 2013. Those at the Kent County Cricket Club, the men who played with and against him, and those old hands back at Ayr Cricket Club, never forgot their favourite son. At Ayr, blokes like the Simpson clan, Ian 'Hank' Johnstone, Derek Thursby and Co. surely raised, as did I, a toast in Mike's memory. Mike played for Ayr and was educated at the Ayr Academy. No doubt he studied the writings of Robert Burns (1759–1796), who wrote a line in his immortal *The Prayer* which really does apply to this gentleman cricketer: 'But thou art good and goodness still.'

Chapter 10

A Royal leg-break

'Hello, Ma'am,' I said rather hesitantly. 'I hope you don't mind, but given you were alone, I thought I should join you.'

Perhaps it was a touch impertinent, and had the Royal presence beside me been Queen Elizabeth I, I may well have been carted off to the Tower for a fate worse than death. It's London, 1972. As a scurry of corgis flitted about her feet, Queen Elizabeth II stood alone by a window in the White Room at Buckingham Palace. No doubt Her Majesty was thinking of how well her invitation to the Australian and England Test cricket teams had gone. Bob Massie, whose Test debut had realised 16 wickets, had completed a demolition job on Ray Illingworth's England team and the match at Lord's finished early on the fourth day. The Royal Household contacted our manager Ray Steele with news that we had been invited to the Palace to meet the Queen and Prince Phillip and partake in cocktails. Teammate Paul Sheahan, our designated driver, screamed past the Grenadier Guardsman, in mid salute, at the sentry box near the Palace gates. Sheahan's splendid driving would have warmed the heart of Mark Webber, Australia's brightest star on the Formula One circuit. The elegant right hand showed no fears as he brought the Ford Executive sedan to a skidding stop on the Buckingham Palace loose pebble driveway in front of the little office where Sir Winston Churchill no doubt waited upon King George VI in the early, dark days of World War II. A man in a dark suit, with matted black hair to match, rushed

A ROYAL LEG-BREAK

to the vehicle, opened the car door and said in condescending tone, 'Ah, you must be some of the Orstralians.'

After meeting the Royals, the players and officials of both teams gathered in a number of circles, offering polite discussion among their select number. I saw the Queen by herself and thought that I should venture to her side and keep her company. Never did I dream of thinking that to join the Queen was anything but good manners; after all I was playing for Australia and Queen Elizabeth was, despite living 12,000 miles away, our Head of State. It didn't seem right to me that the monarch should be left alone. So I slipped away from Ian Chappell, Ross Edwards, Dennis Lillee and Co. and walked straight towards Queen Elizabeth.

My first meeting with Her Majesty Queen Elizabeth II at Lord's, 1968.

What would I say when I got by her side? It seemed that all of the Royal Family were keen on horses and horseracing. Princess Anne was a fine horsewoman. She had become European Champion at three-day eventing a year before I found myself striding across the regal White Room carpet at Buckingham Palace. The Queen stood by a window gazing at the Palace grounds as I moved within earshot. We made eye contact.

'Hello,' she said generously, 'I see you are one of the Australians. How may I help you?' I couldn't bring myself to inform her that I had, in fact, met her four years previously, during the 1968 Australian team's visit to Clarence House, where she had pointed to the Australian Coat of Arms on my tie and made a good guess that I was from the land Down Under.

I decided that I should talk horses, perhaps speak about the vulnerability of a would-be Olympic equestrian who is wholly dependent on the form and the health of their steed. What if such a ride as Princess Anne's horse suffered a broken leg? Just as I pondered such a possibility I stepped back and trod on the front paw of one of the Queen's four corgis, which had been dashing excitedly about the room. The little dog squealed in pain and the Queen looked at me in horror. To my consternation the more I tried to remove myself from the poor dog's paw the more I seemed to drive down on that dear little leg. There was for this clumsy young Australian cricketer no adequate explanation. Not even the most brilliant negotiator or confidence trickster in history could get me out of this spot of bother. I knew the Queen had a good sense of humour. It was 26 June 1972, long after the halcyon days of the great Australian leg-spinners Clarrie Grimmett and Bill O'Reilly, and before Shane Warne emerged on the Test stage. So, thinking quickly, I smilingly declared: 'Ma'am, that's the first genuine leg-break seen in England for more than 30 years!'

Unfortunately my attempt to tease a Royal smile failed miserably. Our meeting came to a rather abrupt halt. The corgis were rounded up and the last I saw all five of them were being ushered into a lift. One of the corgis, who looked familiar, had a decided limp.

Ironically Princess Anne's favourite horse, *Doublet*, broke his leg in a fall in 1974. The Princess was heartbroken and she held the horse as the vet put him down. A year later in 1975 Princess Anne won a silver medal in both individual and team disciplines in the European Eventing Championships in Lulmuhlen, West Germany. She also represented Britain's equestrian team in the 1976 Olympics in Montreal.

Happily I toured England a couple more times after 1972 and was invited to Buckingham Palace on two separate occasions, in 1975 and 1980. The subject of the corgi with the limp was not brought up on either of those occasions.

If my Royal leg-break at Buckingham Palace is not totally forgotten, all, it seems, is forgiven. And if Her Majesty was not amused, I suspect she has taken it all in her stride.

Chapter 11

Rocket Mann: boy wonder of leg-spin bowling

Tony 'Rocket' Mann was the boy wonder of spin bowling. From 1959 to his late teens Tony Mann was the young spin sensation of Western Australian cricket. Those who faced him in his early years will attest to 'Mann's inhumanity to man' by the way he used flight and spin to perplex and befuddle. Like a young Shane Warne, Tony spun his stock leg-break fiercely, such purchase did he achieve that the ball fairly hummed on its dipping trajectory towards the batsman.

By the time both Tony and I were 10 years old we were playing against one another in WA's Under 16 grade competition; Tony for Midland Guildford, me for Mount Lawley. He always bowled from the end at which his father Jack Mann, the umpire, stood. Jack Mann of Houghton Winery was a pioneer in the WA wine industry, creating in 1937 the Houghton White Burgundy, now the White Classic, one of Australia's most popular drops. Jack built a global reputation for excellence at Houghton Winery. He was chief winemaker there from 1937–1974 and was awarded the MBE in 1964.

Umpiring junior cricket was a breeze for Jack. When Tony got a ball to spin and take the edge, or to hit the pads, Jack smiled broadly as if to say 'that's my boy!', and he would gleefully raise the index finger of his left hand.

On weekdays after school Tony, older brother Dorham, younger brother Bill and neighbour Dennis Yagmich played backyard 'Test' matches on the Mann family verandah. Tony bowled, Dorham or Bill batted. Dennis crouched behind the wicket, supposedly there to snare a catch or a stumping but the boys were all too aware that Yagmich's main role was to prevent a ball getting past him and careering on to Angela Mann's patch of prize geraniums. Dennis Yagmich rarely conceded a bye in those verandah Tests. No wonder he went on to keep wicket for WA, then SA.

Before Tony turned 13 he used the orthodox off-break as his variety ball to his stock leggie. At that time, in 1958, he taught himself to bowl the wrong'un and it happened as he experimented on the brick verandah of the family home. That 1958–59 season Tony continued playing senior cricket with Middle Swan, taking 93 wickets and eclipsing the record set by Jack Mann years before.

Jack Mann had been left with a disabled right arm as a legacy of a shooting accident and he was forced to bowl underarm leg-breaks. In the wake of Tony's record-breaking summer for Middle Swan seniors, Midland Guildford stalwarts and WA sporting heroes Keith 'Spud' Slater and Kevin Gartrell called in to see Jack Mann. They were on a mission to coax him into allowing his son to play A grade cricket for Midland Guildford.

'Dad thought I was too young for such a step,' Tony recalled, 'but Spud and Garty were persuasive and Dad finally agreed.'

In his first A grade match for Midland Guildford against a strong Subiaco batting line-up Tony, who played in white shorts, bowled 14 8-ball overs and took 6/29. My Nedlands baseball mentor Neville Pratt, a WA and Australian baseballer and Subiaco's opening bowler, told me: 'That boy Tony Mann will play for Australia. I'm sure of it.'

Next grade game for Midland Guildford, Tony took two cheap wickets against Claremont Cottesloe, the only wickets to fall before the tea break. Wearing his shorts he stood with the other players at the tea pavilion, and the lady pouring the tea from a large container said softly, 'Now, dear, you'll have to wait until the players have finished their afternoon tea.'

Tony can never forget the moment. 'Spud (Slater) took me by the arm and came back to the afternoon tea area and said to the Mrs Wakefield, "Now this fellow Tony Mann is our best bowler. He's earned a well-deserved refreshment."

'Mrs Wakefield and I became very good friends afterwards,' Tony laughed.

At university Tony played alongside John Inverarity and Rod Marsh. Both men saw the genius in young Mann's bowling. It was at university that Tony was given the tag 'Rocket'. Brilliant at cover, Mann had what was known as a rocket arm and the term stuck. So the nickname wasn't a take on Elton John's iconic song after all.

Inverarity said: 'Tony Mann was a brilliant fieldsman. He had a tremendous arm, a rocket arm.' Midland, WA and Test opener Wally Edwards, former Cricket Australia chairman, remembers: 'Tony's father Jack was my first coach and gave me a good start from about the age of 12.

I remember Jack saying "Tony loves to go kangaroo hunting. He is a very good shot and usually only requires one bullet to get the job done. So to give the roos a bit of a chance he doesn't take a gun anymore. He just takes a bag of cricket balls and knocks them over with his bullet throw.'

Rodney Marsh kept to Mann at university and for WA: 'Rocket Mann was a heck of a good leggie in his early days. I would say the fact that he had such a good wrong'un was the start of his demise. He used his wrong'un too often as he knew few could pick it and as a result he lost his excellent leggie. His playing for Baccup in the leagues in England didn't help his bowling either. He would have bowled with a wet ball and just tried to contain. The last I remember him bowling in Sheffield Shield cricket he still had the wrong'un but his leggie wasn't really threatening. What a shame! Batsmen eventually realised the difference between his leggie and his wrong'un as the different ball was his leg-break!'

In the early 1960s, near the end of his career, Neil Harvey batted for an invitation side against the WA Governor's XI at the WACA. Tony deceived Harvey with a beautifully flighted wrong'un, which dipped sharply and the ball spun away from the great left-hander with Harvey stranded well down the wicket and Marsh joyfully whipped off the bails.

That was some coup for the youngster. Despite Harvey always charging well down the track to the spinners, he had never before been stumped in any of his 137 Test innings, many of which were against the wiles of fabulous slow bowlers such as Jim Laker, Tony Lock, Sonny Ramadhin, Lance Gibbs and Hugh Tayfield.

The years flew by and Tony started bowling more wrong'uns than leg breaks. Marsh, Inverarity and ex-WA all-rounder Ian Brayshaw are at one about the Mann wrong'un. They believe, as do I, that Rocket's heavy dependence on the wrong'un was detrimental to his wicket-taking capabilities. Yet Rocket himself has no regrets about the way he went about his bowling. Maybe Stuart MacGill got things right. MacGill had a superb wrong'un in his armory, but he used it wisely and it became a brilliantly effective shock weapon for him. Those who saw Mann the boy, the boy wonder of leg-spin bowling, ponder what might have been had Tony used his wrong'un sparingly during his career.

Even so, Rocket Mann was a very good first-class cricketer for WA, playing 80 matches, scoring 2544 runs at 24.22 and taking 200 wickets at 34.54 runs apiece. His best of five 5-wicket hauls was his 6/94 for WA against SA on the Adelaide Oval.

And wouldn't you know, he trapped me plumb lbw with his wrong'un!

Rocket played four Tests for Australia against India Down Under in 1977–78, a series played in fierce opposition to Kerry Packer's World Series Cricket. He took just 4/316 at an average of 79, but it was his 105 in Perth which highlighted his brief Test career. Rocket went in at the fall of the first wicket, becoming the second nightwatchman in Test history, after Pakistan's Nasim-ul-Ghani, to score a century. He never got to bowl the Bunny Gartell (Kevin Gartrell's father) special the 'Midland Hanger', a ball which W.G. Grace so successfully lobbed all those years ago. The Midland Hanger, a high-flung delivery, was designed to land squarely on the top of the bails.

'I probably did bowl the odd Midland Hanger ... but never on purpose!' Tony laughed.

He was lucky to have come under the influence of Slater and Gartrell, and later Norm O'Neill and Barry Richards, all of whom gave such great service to Midland Guildford CC.

There was a time when Tony Lock coached a group of 12 spinners in a special squad at the WACA Ground. Among that 12 were four men who went on to play Test cricket: myself (as an off-spinner), leg-spinner Terry Jenner, left-arm spinner John Inverarity, and Tony Mann.

Throughout his cricket career Rocket Mann batted, bowled and fielded with such obvious joy and never-ending enthusiasm.

He was the best young spinner of my experience.

Chapter 12

England in Australia 1907–08: a baggageman's inside story

Bill 'Fergie' Ferguson ruled the roost as baggageman-scorer for the Australian Cricket team from 1905 to 1957. Known as 'Mr Cricket' long before Mike Hussey's parents were born, Fergie also worked for the England, South African and New Zealand Test touring teams.

He became a fixture, but he was upstaged. Once.

North Haven postmaster Ken Riches has brought the amazing tale to light. How Ken's grandfather, Frederick William Hickman Riches, was appointed baggageman for England's 1907-08 touring team Down Under is some tale.

Fred Riches was born in England in 1886 and at the age of 14 he joined the merchant navy. He remained in the merchant navy until 1907, serving on a variety of famous liners before he finally landed the plum job of captain's servant and steward on the SS *Ophir*, the very vessel that carried the England team to Australia in the early summer of 1907-08. Thankfully Fred kept a diary and his grandson passed along copies. Almost immediately after the SS *Ophir* berthed in Sydney, Fred received a telegram from Major Trevor, the England team manager: 'I thought it was a fine chance to see the country, catching the first train to Adelaide whereupon I met Captain Arthur Jones at the South Australian Hotel and began duties straight away.' After their first match at the Adelaide Oval, Fred had to arrange the forwarding of the team's luggage to the Melbourne Express for the upcoming game against Victoria at the MCG.

'The game against South Australia ended at 3 pm. The luggage weighed 28 cwt (a tad over 1400 kg). The instant Fred alighted from the train in Melbourne there was, he suspected, some jiggery-pokery at play.

'A man showed me a letter stating that he was authorised to take the luggage.' Fred told them there was no use their waiting as a carrier had been engaged. 'They left in a huff, whispering among themselves. Later I saw a man "mistaking" his bag for one of the cricketers and after a little discussion he reluctantly handed the bag over.'

Fred was beginning to learn all about a Test tour. On the train trip from Melbourne to Sydney for the next match, 'a gentleman pointed out to me from a station called Glenrowan where Ned Kelly made his last stand. It looked to be a very wild spot and not by any means a nice place to be after dark'. In Sydney the team lunched aboard the warship, HMS *Powerful*, enduring a severe thunderstorm, then boarded the train for the 29-hour train ride to Brisbane. '(SF) Barnes and (Joe) Hardstaff – amusingly called "Hotstuff" were favourites among the England team.'

One of the youngsters in the party, Jack Hobbs debuted at the MCG in January 1908, scoring 83 and 28 in an imposing start to his 61-Test career. This match was the lone Test England won in the series; they lost the other four. It was no ordinary match for England's ninth wicket fell at 243 when Arthur Fielder joined S.F. Barnes at the wicket. In the dressing room Fred Riches noted the tense faces of the batting side. Wilfred Rhodes lounged comfortably smoking a pipe and George Gunn, who had been reading the daily broadsheet, sat up his eyes glued to the action in the middle. There was total silence as Barnes and Fielder gradually pegged back the score.

The target for victory was 282. Eventually after an hour of nail-biting tension, the scores drew level. One run to win; one wicket and it's a tie. Barnes figured that the Australian captain Warwick Armstrong would continue his defensive ploy of leg-theory. So Barnes backed away to the next ball and hit it to the right of Gerry Hazlitt in the covers. To his horror Barnes, a tough Lancastrian without airs and graces, noticed that Fielder was standing still at the other end. 'For God's sake, Pip. Get off boom man and run!'

Fielder was yards out of his ground when Hazlitt threw wildly and the ball flew way over keeper Hanson Carter's head. The Australian gloveman, an undertaker who often drove

his horse-drawn hearse to Paddington grade matches, knew the instant Hazlitt released the ball that their efforts to prevent the England victory charge was dead and buried.

Oh that the ball went to either Victor Trumper or Clem Hill, both gun fieldsmen.

In the 1909 edition of *Wisden* it was drolly noted: 'The result could be equally attributed to "A. Fielder" and "a fielder". Alas, Jack Hobbs' first Test match would have been Test cricket's first tie.

'Before we went down the mine we were given overalls and old boots. It was funny to see the cricketers in such dirty clothes. Despite the weight of the old hat and clothes were all were prepared to go 1500 feet below the surface of the earth.

'There was excitement. We each held a lighted candle. Three of the team went down first in a sort of box, hanging on a wire hawser and packed like sardines. We soon followed the others down in the hanging box. With our lighted candles all was fine until the foul air put out our candles. Everything was in darkness.'

The party soon became lost in the dark tunnels, not a peep out of a canary.

'After crawling through cramped, wet nooks and crannies we soon arrived back at the shaft and thankfully we were soon on top in daylight. It was still raining. A photographer sat patiently near the opening of the shaft. His photograph appeared in a Bendigo illustrated newspaper, the *Bendigoian*.

Fred Riches' experience with the England touring team delighted him. He saw much of Australia and fell in love with the place. He proved diligent in his job. There was the time certain dodgy types tried to swipe the players' luggage in Melbourne; the heart-racing descent in the gold mine; the umpire smoking his pipe on the field in Hobart. As the team departed Adelaide for Fremantle and the voyage home to Blighty, Fred wrote his final entry in the diary. After checking the luggage aboard the ship *Mooltan*, 'I had finished my duties with the team'.

A few days earlier, Fred received a note (dated 5 March 1908) from Major Phillip Trevor, the England team manager, which said (in part): 'I found him willing, strictly honest and sober and always at his post. I can recommend him for employment which requires such qualities.'

The Test tour experience had him hooked on the land Down Under. Fred migrated to Adelaide in 1908, first residing at 71 Norwood Parade. He never returned to the Old Dart. He married Isabel Baylis in Norwood in 1909 and joined the SA Railways. Stationed in various parts of SA from 1911–1949, including Gladstone where he took up Australian Rules Football, playing in their 1913 premiership, Fred was stationed in Peake in the Mallee, then Penola before becoming station master at Largs Bay Railway Station in 1935, a position he held until retirement in July 1949.

In March 1913, Fred received a letter (below, in part) from England Test batsman Jack Hobbs in response to a letter he had written to him.

Windsor
Alexander Street, Largs
15 January 1913

Dear Fred,
I was glad to learn that you are still alive and kicking, and also that you are a full-blown Station Master.

Of course I remember you quite well and although it is a long time since we had that tour together I have often wondered what had happened to you. Little did I think then that I would make another five trips out there, but I must say that I have enjoyed them all and I shall hope to come again for I have a great number of friends out here.

My wife and I are staying with friends here (in Largs Bay) and I am afraid there is little chance of our getting over to Glenelg.

However, I hope to have the pleasure of meeting you again before I leave for home.

Yours sincerely
Jack Hobbs

(Apparently Fred Riches, who lived in Largs for years, must have been temporarily living in Glenelg at the time Hobbs was in Largs. He had sailed from England to Australia, but the pony and trap ride from Largs to Glenelg ... too much!)

In 2000, the five greatest cricketers of the 20th century, as judged by a panel of 100 people commissioned by *Wisden* was named: Don Bradman, Garry Sobers, Jack Hobbs, Shane Warne and Viv Richards. To Fred the letter from Jack Hobbs was like receiving a missive from one of the game's 'immortals' – cricketing Royalty indeed.

Hobbs was to amass 61,237 first-class runs with 197 centuries. He scored more than 100 centuries after turning 40. He was the first England professional cricketer to be knighted, in 1953 aged 71.

And Fred Riches, who held the plum job of baggageman and dressing-room attendant for the visiting England Test team for one glorious Australian summer, is now part of the rich tapestry which makes up the special fabric of the game of cricket. Fred Riches was by no means a cricket immortal. He was nonetheless an integral, important part of that unsung band of helpers behind the scenes in that England cricket team of long ago.

Chapter 13

That elusive image

There is a cricketing heaven after all.

After a slap-up meal at the SA Tattersalls Club in Grenfell Street, I found myself standing alongside the Walking Wisden. To my left was the greatest batsman of them all, Don Bradman, and to my right was South Australia's greatest all-round sportsman, Victor Richardson.

A record five SA cricketers were selected for the 1968 tour of England – Eric Freeman, Ian Chappell, Barry Jarman, Neil Hawke and me. What publication that photo appeared in I know not, but somehow a faded, grainy newspaper image turned up in an old scrapbook of mine. I knew that the original photograph hung for years on a wall of the Tattersalls Club members dining room and bar. In 1977 the club was sold to Don Evangelista, who used five floors of the building, but locked the door of the old room and bar.

This Adelaide time capsule sported the original carpet, the magnificent long oak bar, all lighting and fittings: a magnificent room which reflected the opulence, prestige and riches of old Adelaide. It wasn't until 2012 that two entrepreneurial businessmen, Grant Mollison and Marcus Benardi, approached Don Evangelista with the idea of staging events in the room.

In town one day a friend suggested I try Harry's Bar in Grenfell Street for lunch.

'It was once the Tattersalls Club. You'll love it ... and you will delight in the memorabilia.'

Memorabilia? I climbed the stairs to Harry's Bar. The room was just as I remembered it; gently traditional, lavish. Straight away I focused on a large black-and-white photograph adorning the western wall. I stood transfixed. Grant Mollison said the photograph was a great find.

'When Marcus and I had the room cleaned we looked in the attic and there we discovered old newspapers and some photographs, one of Queen Elizabeth II and the one you were seeking.'

Grant kindly allowed me to take the original photograph away and have it copied and I posted copies to Chappelli, Jar, Fritz and Les Favell's son, Alan.

Harry's Bar is brilliant: today it is one of best haunts for lunch and dinner in Adelaide.

There are some extraordinary links to the SA Tattersalls Club. In 1867 the Duke of Edinburgh (Prince Alfred not Prince Phillip) visited Adelaide. Interested in meeting sporting men over a glass of wine at the Tattersalls Club, he was disappointed that no such club yet existed in Adelaide. The Duke held his meeting at the Globe Hotel in Rundle Street instead.

Later that year the Prince selected a cricket team from officers serving on his ship, the *Galatea*. Prince Alfred's XI played a game of cricket in Sydney against a team of Indigenous men, most of whom were picked in the famous 1868 Aboriginal cricket tour of England. At the match the Prince befriended some of the Australians and told them if they got to England he would come to see them play. In March 1868, the Duke narrowly survived an attempt on his life at a gala picnic in Clontarf and, nursing two gunshot flesh wounds, he sailed home to England.

True to his word he was present at one of the 47 two-day games the Aboriginals played in England, and the Duke personally handed each of the Australian players a crisp ten shilling note.

The SA Tattersalls Club was formed in 1880. Due to strict gaming laws and falling membership it closed in 1887. A year later Parliament passed a Totalizator Bill and Tattersalls was resurrected. The club eventually bought Grenfell Chambers on Grenfell Street and built clubrooms in 1917. In the

1970s women were admitted as members for the first time. But time had run out for both the club's male and female membership. In 1977 the Tattersalls Club foundered and the building was sold. And my hunt for the original photograph began.

Chapter 14

'Please, Mr Stoddart'

They called it the miracle match of cricket's Golden Age. Late in the SCG first Test of December 1894, Australia was in the box seat to force first blood in the series. Australia had batted first and thanks to George Giffen (161) and Syd Gregory (201) the hosts made a mammoth 586. England scored 325 in reply and was forced to follow on. Despite England's better effort in the second dig (437), Australia needed just 177 runs in its second innings to win. You could bet London to a brick on an Australian victory.

Late on the sixth day of the match heavy clouds enveloped the ground. But no rain fell until the heavens opened up in the wee hours. And how it rained. Overnight Sydney experienced a wild thunderstorm. Torrential rain hit the city with tremendous force. Gutters and drains overflowed and the streets were awash.

The next day dawned hot and glorious. However, in those days of yore Australian groundsmen produced uncovered wickets and the heat of the sun burning down on the sodden surface of the SCG wicket created what was called a 'sticky dog', a devil of a track where the ball tended to stop in the mud on occasion or rear like a striking cobra on another. It made batting impossible for those who followed a technically correct path and couldn't or wouldn't adapt. A few years later Victor Trumper became a master of making runs on such wickets and against good quality bowling. But that

'PLEASE, MR STODDART'

came later. On the seventh and final day of the 1894 Test the Australian batting was about to experience the unpredictability of the 'sticky dog'.

Key England bowlers, Johnny Briggs and Booby Peel, both left-arm orthodox spinners, had downed a few pints and whatever else before the storm hit. They must have been convinced that an Australian victory was sure. 'Under the circumstances, what harm was there to have a few?'

Briggs and Peel woke a little worse for wear. A couple of hours later, under a blazing sun and still clad in their civilian clobber, Briggs and Peel sauntered out on to the middle of the SCG to inspect the wicket. There was little evidence of an overnight storm having hit the ground; that is until the pair reached the square. Bobby stared hard and quizzically at the wicket, before stooping over to get a closer look. He bent his knees and pressed the turf with his index finger.

Peel stood to his full height and whispered to Johnny, 'Somebody's bin waterin' wicket in neight. We'll 'ave 'em out in a jiffy!'

By the time the pair returned to the pavilion to shed their serge and watch chains and don their creams, they were still clearly a little unsteady on their feet. England captain Andrew Stoddart was particularly angry about Bobby Peel's condition: 'Good Lord, man. You're drunk. A damned disgrace to yourself and your country!'

And with that the skipper grabbed Peel by the scruff of the neck and stuck him under the showers to sober him up. After which Peel, gradually shedding the effects of the demon drink the night before, realised that the 'sticky dog' of a wicket was tailor-made for him and his spin partner.

'Give me the ball, Mr Stoddart, and I'll get t'boogers out before loonch!'

Peel 6/67 and Briggs 3/25 ran through the Australians like a packet of Epsom Salts and from a comfortable position of 2/130, the home side crashed to be all out for 166. England had won by 10 runs.

Chapter 15

Have two and that will do

In 1969 India had a population of a shade fewer than 542 million. Indira Gandhi was then prime minister and along with other moves to quell the rate of the nation's population explosion she championed the concept of placing an important advertisement on page two of the Indian telephone book. If you turned to page two you would have found the impressive advertisement which said it all: HAVE TWO AND THAT WILL DO.

If a married man had two children then agreed to have a government-funded vasectomy he would receive as his reward a transistor radio. To a cricket fan – and aren't all Indians cricket fans? – a transistor radio would be invaluable to keep up-to-date with the state of play at all times, whether you were at the ground or not.

In the November 1969 first Test at Bombay (now Mumbai), we had India on the ropes at 8/125 in their innings before all hell broke loose. At a vital part of the Indian second innings, Indian skipper Ajit Wadekar, who hit a splendid 46, and tailender Srinivasaraghavan Venkataraghavan ('Venkat') were resisting all that was thrown at them and they lasted nearly an hour to frustrate the Australians. Then came the vital delivery, which changed the match and was the catalyst for the riot to follow. Venkat tried to cut fast-medium bowler Alan Connolly. There was a noise but the Indian missed the ball by a mile. To the amusement of keeper Brian Taber and first slipper Ian

Chappell, Victorian Keith Stackpole roared an appeal from gully and umpire Pan raised his index finger.

Radio commentator Devraj Puri was livid. He told the masses, many of whom must have read the advertisement on page two of the phone book and had their brand new trannies pressed to their ears. Mr Puri told his listeners that Venkat was not out and that Australia was not playing the game in a gentlemanly fashion, a clear indication that he thought Venkat had been cheated. Already there was a serious problem for administrators and security staff at Brabourne Stadium. Tickets had been forged and in many spots two fans were fighting over the one available seat. However, it was the commentator's comments that most infuriated spectators.

In the outer deck chairs were stacked high and set alight. A thick pall of smoke enveloped the ground. Next door the tennis club was on fire and nearby parked cars were ablaze.

Then came the bottle throwing. Some 5000 bottles littered the outfield. Fans were trying to tear down the high cyclone wire fence and invade the pitch. Police swarmed the ground and pleaded with captain Bill Lawry to take his men off the field. Lawry refused and whispered to Ian Chappell, 'Jeez, we need a wicket badly.'

Connolly fancied his chance of a wicket bowling to any batsman in the smoky haze. The police got the fans off the fence by picking up the bottles on the field and throwing them at spectators.

Suddenly a little man dashed onto the ground. Lawry waved him away. 'No, Mr Lawry. There is too much smoke. I am the official scorer and I cannot see the play. I am going home.' And with that Jehangir Irani, his precious scorebook under his arm, scurried away. We later learnt that all was well for Mr Puri, the radio man who incited fans and was largely responsible for the riot with his comments on air, was to become the official scorer from the time Mr Irani went missing until stumps were drawn.

At stumps John Gleeson copped a bottle to the back of the head. When we arrived in the dressing room we found an exhausted 12th man Eric Freeman seated on a bench. He had had a torrid battle protecting our gear, and the room was strewn with broken glass.

Later Fritz Freeman had a close call in Calcutta when the team bus was stoned. A cricket-ball-sized rock smashed through the bus window only inches from his head. But that incident came weeks later.

Maybe Doug Walters had had a premonition about the day (the fourth day of the match) for he stacked the bath in the team room full of cans of beer and covered the lot in ice. Given the stadium, where we were housed, was partially on fire and there was pandemonium downstairs we barricaded the room that Doug had fortified in more ways than one and settled back. An hour later our manager Fred Bennett somehow got through the barricade and said in a breathless voice: 'Fellas, there are 10,000 people downstairs baying for Lawry's blood.'

Walters slowly stood, taking a sip of beer, and said: 'Hand Bill Lawry over to the mob, Fred, and let's get on with the drinking!'

Postscript: All the carefully laid plans to prevent the continuing population explosion, including the Gandhi Government's idea to give those who underwent a vasectomy operation a new transistor radio, failed. By 2017 India's population had reached 1.34 billion, up from the 542 million in 1969, the year of that splendid page two advertisement in the Indian telephone book. Three years on and the population is hardly abating.

Chapter 16

CHO

The year is 1950 and 12-year-old Johnny Gleeson picked up an illustrated article about the finger-flicking Australian Test bowler Jack Iverson. He was dubbed the 'mystery spinner' because England's Ashes squad of that 1950–51 summer were bemused and puzzled by his bizarre spinning craft. To the Englishmen this chap Iverson was a veritable 'Mr Magic', a seeming off break turned from the leg and what appeared to be a leg-break came back into the right-hander. Iverson took 21 wickets at 15.73 in that series before treading on a ball in the Adelaide Test, hobbling through the fifth match and never playing big cricket again.

But his finger-flicking mystery bowling style immediately held great fascination for young Gleeson, whose long slender fingers were ideal for spinning a ball, and especially well-suited to the folded finger grip used by Iverson.

Gleeson began his cricketing life as a wicketkeeper and when he moved from Tamworth to Sydney with the PMG in 1956 he kept in the lower grades for Western Suburbs. In secret he trained alone, trying to master the finger-flick bowling.

In 1958, at the age of 20, Gleeson returned to Tamworth. He won selection for an overseas tour of Canada with The Emu Club. Frustrated that his bowlers couldn't make inroads in the opposition batting Gleeson shed the pads and first began to bowl his 'Iverson' style.

He first bowled in a serious match in Melbourne in 1964, turning out for the Australian Postal Institute. His captain was Tom Brooks, former NSW fast bowler and Test umpire. His deliveries mystified all and sundry that day; many deliveries beating the bat and the wicketkeeper. By the summer of 1965-66 Gleeson was the first-choice spinner for Gunnedah. Jack Chegwin, a great promoter of country cricket in NSW, took sides festooned with current and ex-Test cricketers to the outlying areas, ever on the lookout for raw talent.

Gleeson took wickets in the match and delighted in getting the chance to bowl to Richie Benaud, one of his boyhood heroes. Benaud knew exciting talent when he saw it and he took a big interest in Gleeson, advising him to join the Balmain Club, which had Fred Bennett as its secretary, a man destined to one day become chairman of the Australian Cricket Board.

Gleeson got bags of wickets for Balmain and in 1966-67 he made his debut for NSW at the WACA Ground in Perth. He bowled 23 overs into the wind, known as the 'Fremantle Doctor', but Gleeson found operating on the hard, true surface at the WACA less than great. He took one wicket and was made to carry the drinks in the next match in Adelaide.

Sir Donald Bradman, then chairman of the Test selectors, met NSW captain Brian Booth on the eve of the match and asked him who was going to be 12th man.

'Johnny Gleeson,' Booth said confidently.

'Well, that's the first mistake you've made this game.'

Bradman always made it his business to know all about emerging players. He well-remembered how Iverson had bamboozled Freddie Brown's Englishmen and he wondered whether this bloke Gleeson could do a similar job on Ray Illingworth's team down the track. When NSW batted Sir Donald asked Gleeson if he would like to accompany him to the nets and bowl to him. Bradman was then aged 58. He wore neither pads nor gloves, but half-a-dozen balls from Gleeson was enough for him to say, 'Thanks, John. By the end of the season I think you'll be playing for Australia.'

Gleeson toured New Zealand with an Australian Second XI in 1967 and by December of the same year he made his Test debut against India. He played in all four Tests, taking the last three wickets in the third Test to help Australia win by 39 runs.

Gleeson was a certain selection for England in 1968. He was dubbed 'CHO' (Cricket Hours Only) – apart from the nets or at the ground CHO was never there. Maybe he wanted to maintain the mystery.

CHO revelled in the mystery. He was very much the man of the moment. We arrived at the Waldorf Hotel, our London home away from home, with Lawry talking about playing bright cricket ('so long as we win') and CHO fast asleep in the background, his head resting on 'Garth' McKenzie's broad right shoulder.

I roomed with CHO in 1968 and one day asked how the publicity affected him.

'Doesn't worry me in the slightest,' he said. 'Never read the newspapers.'

Next I found him trying to close the lid on a suitcase filled to overflowing with newspaper cuttings of one mystery finger-flick bowler John Gleeson. He had the dry quirky sense of humour of a bushie based in Outback Australia long ago.

By 1968 Bill Lawry had taken over from Bob Simpson as Test captain. Lawry liked to keep runs at bay. He managed his fast and medium-paced attack brilliantly. When it came to spin, Lawry could play it well, but he didn't understand spinners. However, Lawry did like the way Gleeson bowled. CHO operated with a flat trajectory and was more at home on a green-top than a slow, dusty turner, thus complementing the likes of the fast men Graham McKenzie, Alan Connolly, Neil Hawke and their ilk.

CHO didn't set the world on fire in India in 1969. Apart from the Bombay (Mumbai) Test, where the wicket had bounce and pace, Gleeson struggled to make an impact.

He made an impact of a different sort on the last day of our match against South Zone at Bangalore. Set 200 runs to get in two hours 50 minutes we collapsed to the masterly spin of Erapally Prasanna, who by the fall of our sixth wicket had the incredible figures of 6/9 off nine overs. Barnacle Bill Lawry was battling out for a draw at the other end when CHO strolled to the wicket with the air of a man without a care in the world. At square leg he spoke quietly to umpire B.N. Nagaraj before heading straight down the wicket to chat to the official at Prasanna's end, umpire N.S. Rishi.

That done CHO leant over his bat, rejecting the umpire's request to take guard, quipping, 'Not required, Mr Umpire. I took guard in Bombay weeks ago.'

While Lawry defended stoically, Gleeson either padded away or hit out. Stumps were drawn five minutes before the scheduled close because a section of the crowd began throwing stones. Lawry had batted for all 52 overs for an unconquered 10, CHO was not out 18 and Australia at stumps was 8/90.

There were back slaps all round for Barnacle Bill and CHO, but Ian Chappell, Doug Walters and Company were far more interested in what CHO said to the umpires.

'Well I said to the ump at square leg: "Mr Umpire if you give me out lbw I will wrap this bat about your head ... and I said the same thing to the other umpire."'

In my mind's eye I can see CHO now. He moves in with a funny gait, a bit like a comical mix of Groucho Marx and Ronnie Corbett. He's not a short man, but stays low. The delivery doesn't make a fizzing sound like a Prasanna or a Shane Warne. It glides out of that folded finger grip, always on target but devoid of what we call 'loop' or 'shape'. The unknowing batsman is easily snared by CHO, who really was a master of deceit with the cricket ball. Even if the ball went as straight as a gun barrel his body language was a disarming distraction for the unwary batsman.

Probably his crowning glory was his Test bowling against South Africa in 1970. The South Africans had a powerful batting line-up. headed by Graeme Pollock, Barry Richards, Eddie Barlow and Mike Procter. Only Richards could play Gleeson effectively. When asked by others, including his teammates, Richards would say: 'If you go after it and hit the ball just as it lands it matters not which way the ball turns.'

Barlow tried that very thing against CHO in the third Test at Johannesburg, didn't quite get to the pitch of the ball and Brian Taber politely whipped off the bails with the man they called 'Bunter' yards short of his ground.

In the four Tests Gleeson bowled 255 overs against the South Africans, taking 19 wickets at 38.94. He bowled a good deal better than his figures reflect. His bowling mystified many a good batsmen and Ray Illingworth's 1970–71 Ashes squad was no exception. In the SCG fourth Test John Edrich waltzed up the pitch for a mid-wicket chat with his opening partner, Geoff Boycott.

'Hey, Boycs,' Edrich said joyfully, 'I've just worked out Gleeson. I know for sure where each one's going.'

'Oh, is that all, Ede,' Boycott laughed, 'I worked CHO out two Tests ago … but don't tell those boogers in the dressing-room.'

John Gleeson was a great character. He spoke with passion about bowling, especially spin bowling, and the mystery of the finger-flicking style. Just as he loved the Iverson way, CHO delighted in Arjantha Mendis' similar finger-flicking style. He proved to us all that some wicketkeepers can turn their hand successfully to spin bowling. CHO certainly turned heads with his style. And to have the then chairman of Australia's Test selectors Sir Donald Bradman in your corner, even before you have played a first-class game, is quite something.

Chapter 17

The first 'Mankad' in Tests

It is now more than 70 years since the first 'Mankad' in Test match cricket had fans at the SCG in uproar. On a December day in 1947, having bowled India out for 188 in its first innings, the Australian openers Arthur Morris and Bill Brown took the score to 28 when left-arm spinner Vinoo Mankad stopped in his delivery stride and whipped the bails off at the non-striker's end. Brown had moved down the pitch too quickly and was clearly out of his ground when Mankad struck. Opinion was divided among spectators. Given that Mankad had done the honourable thing by warning Brown in the India–Australia XI match a few weeks before and Brown had not heeded the warning and lost his wicket in the self-same fashion, Mankad, albeit years later, won approval from an unlikely source.

With the forlorn Brown meandering his way to the dressing-room, Australian captain Don Bradman joined Morris. No doubt they briefly discussed the incident at the wicket, but Bradman did not make public comment until years later when the matter was dealt with in his in his autobiography, *Farewell to Cricket*:

> for the life of me I can't understand why [the press] questioned his sportsmanship. The Laws of Cricket make it quite clear that the non-striker must keep within his ground until the ball has been delivered. If not, why is the provision there which enables the bowler to run him out? By backing

up too far or too early, the non-striker is very obviously gaining an unfair advantage.

While the 'Mankading' of Brown was perfectly legal, the action was considered unsporting in the extreme by a furious Australian media. For more years than the locusts have eaten, there has been something of an 'unwritten law' among cricketers that a non-striker must be warned that he is transgressing, or taking unfair advantage by backing up too far, at least once before running a player out. Mankad had warned Brown in a previous match, and the batsman ignored the warning. In the Test match there was no such warning.

It was as simple as this: Brown once again transgressed, taking what Bradman and thousands of others thought to be an 'unfair advantage', so Mankad stopped at delivery and snapped the bails off in an instant. Brown was fairly and legitimately out; Mankad was instantly coloured the villain of the piece.

The 'Mankad' has become part of cricket lore. While many deplore 'Mankading', the great Indian all-rounder's action was entirely within the laws of cricket. And unlike the underarm incident in the Australia–New Zealand ODI at the MCG in 1981, Mankad's action did not contravene the Spirit of Cricket.

In Test matches there have been three other 'Mankads': New Zealand's Ewan Chatfield ran out Derek Randall at Christchurch in 1978; Australia's Alan Hurst 'Mankaded' Pakistan's Sikander Bakht at the WACA in 1979, and at the Adelaide Oval in January 1969 West Indian Charlie Griffith demolished the stumps at the non-striker's end with Australia's Ian Redpath wandering down the track, yards out of his ground and oblivious to the danger.

Early this year there was a sensational incident in the Under-19 World Cup. Zimbabwe needed just 3 runs in the last over to win the match and make the quarter finals. Non-striker Richard Ngarare was standing outside the popping crease, with his bat on the line. Fast man Keemo Paul approached the crease in his run up, stopped and smashed the stumps. The umpires asked the West Indians whether they wanted to withdraw their appeal, but they didn't. The non-striker was ruled out and Zimbabwe lost their chance to play in the quarter finals. In this case, there did seem contravention of the spirit of the game, because the batsman was simply unaware. He wasn't knowingly taking an advantage.

***

Vinoo Mankad's memory should not be sullied by the incident with Bill Brown that December day at the SCG in 1947. Born Mulvantrai Himmatlal Mankad, he became known as Vinoo Mankad and was an ever popular member of the Indian side from 1946–1959. In 44 Test matches Mankad scored 2109 runs at 31.47 with five hundreds, his 231 versus New Zealand at Chennai in 1955–56 his best and the highest by an Indian at the time. This record was only broken in 1983, after Sunil Gavaskar made 236 against the West Indies. In the same innings against New Zealand, Mankad and his opening partner Pankaj Roy recorded the highest opening partnership of 413 runs, a record that stood for 52 years. This record was only broken by South African pair Neil McKenzie and Graeme Smith, who put on 415 runs for the first wicket against Bangladesh in 2008.

In Tests, Mankad took 162 wickets at an average of 32.32 and his most famous all-round performance came at Lord's against England in 1952. On the first day of the game, Mankad opened the batting, scoring 72. He then bowled a marathon 73 overs, taking 5/196. Batting a second time Mankad hit a brilliant 184 in just under five hours of grit, concentration and deft placement. England won the match, but by the time the hosts claimed victory on the last day, Mankad's bowling figures read 97–36–231–5. Nobody in cricket history had spent more time on the field in a Lord's Test match. The game lasted exactly 24 hours and 35 minutes of which Mankad spent 18 hours 45 minutes in the middle. He bowled 24 overs in the England second innings, 12 of them maidens, operating against such luminaries as Peter May, Denis Compton and Len Hutton. Fleet Street acclaimed 'Mankad the Magnificent' and 'England vs Mankad Now'.

Alex Bannister wrote in the *Daily Mail*: 'Keith Miller, acknowledged as the world's top all-rounder, has never done as much in a single match as has Mankad in this Test.'

In the Indian summer of 1937–38, while ominous clouds gathered over Europe, the 20-year-old Vinoo Mankad played five 'unofficial Tests' against

THE FIRST 'MANKAD' IN TESTS

Lord Tennyson's touring side. He headed both the batting and bowling averages: 62.66 with the bat and 14.53 with the ball. The young all-rounder so impressed Lord Tennyson that he said Mankad would readily get a place in a World Eleven. Then war intervened and Mankad had to wait until 1946 to play his first Test for India.

Throughout his career Mankad excelled. But the stigma of his controversial dismissal of Bill Brown lingers in the minds and memories of many.

The first known instance of a 'Mankad' came during an impromptu cricket match on the Victorian goldfields in 1853, a year before the infamous Eureka Stockade miners' uprising. Gold seekers came from all parts of the world; some were university graduates from Oxford and Cambridge. Indeed a cricket match was arranged between a team from Oxford (the Dark Blues) and Cambridge (the Light Blues) on a field near Ballarat. In the wake of the game, a description of an 'incident' in the match was printed in some obscure publication by the author who went by the pseudonym the 'Old Fogey'.

Oxford was all out for 43. Cambridge was 3/20 when in walked a stout fellow who could run like a hare and wield the willow with some style. The Old Fogey takes up the story:

> The old Cantab revealed as correct play as could be shown on our peculiar wicket and the score increased to 35. Here a crisis occurred. One of the batsman, not the Cantab, you may be sure, was very eager in backing up, and once when at my end he overshot the mark before the ball was delivered, and, I turning suddenly, knocked the stumps flying while the batsman was fully a foot out of his ground. The umpire of course gave him out, and the batsman made tracks for the tent. The crowd, however, shouted out 'swindle', and several stopped the batsman and told him to go back.
>
> The hum of voices soon swelled into a deafening roar. Oh! what a row, what a rumpus, what a rioting it was to be sure. After a lengthy explanation, it was admitted by all that player was out. Then the wild excitement died gradually away; the game was resumed, and harmony and pleasantness reigned once more.

Chapter 18

Lillee the firebrand

On a typically hot Adelaide January day in 1971, Dennis Lillee burst on to the international cricket scene with one hell of a bang. Despite England scoring a first innings 470 on a pitch as flat as a pancake, the young firebrand bowled with amazing speed and accuracy to pick up 5/84 off 28.3 overs.

Thanks to a fighting 202-run second-wicket stand by Keith Stackpole (136) and Ian Chappell (104), Australia managed to draw the match. While the game marked Lillee's entry into big cricket, it proved to be captain Bill Lawry's final Test match. He was immediately replaced by Ian Chappell, whose captaincy was destined to mould a tremendous team in the 1970s, one to compare with any in the modern era.

Born on 28 July 1949 (and sharing his birthdate with other famous folk including Nelson Mandela, Richard Branson and cricket's legendary W.G. Grace) in the Perth suburb of Subiaco to Keith and Shirley Lillee, Dennis developed a keen sense of loyalty and determination early in his life. A truck driver, Keith Lillee was often home late of an evening and although dog-tired he was always keen to bowl a few down in the backyard to his boys, Dennis and his younger brother Trevor. After a brilliant tour of England in 1972, where Lillee took 31 wickets (eclipsing Clarrie Grimmett's long-standing record of 29 wickets for an Australian in an Ashes series) signs of back trouble began to emerge. Team masseur Dave 'Doc' McErlane worked on Lillee's back for days on end during that long tour. The back strain – as he thought it was – became a major concern for him when Pakistan toured Australia in 1972–73.

Lillee toured West Indies late in that summer, but broke down after one Test match. Many believed Lillee's career was all but over when he sustained multiple stress fractures of his back. He underwent a long regime of intensive physiotherapy under the direction of Dr Frank Pyke, a Perth club cricketer, baseballer and footballer. Frank's son, Don Pyke, later coached the Adelaide Crows in the Australian Football League.

Lillee's determination became legend, when he returned to big cricket in 1974–75 – perfect timing to partner Jeff Thomson against England Down Under when the speed pair destroyed the visiting team; Australia winning 4–1. Lillee and Thomson were magnificent that summer. Thommo with his hurricane pace and Lillee with the guile of a good spinner at high speed had England on toast in this fiery Ashes summer. Cartoonist Paul Rigby summed it up best with this award-winning cartoon, which appeared in all News Ltd newspapers across the land.

Good judges describe Dennis Lillee as the 'complete bowler', a cricketer who always kept one step ahead of the pack. On the Test arena, Lillee was never beaten. West Indian champion Viv Richards took the sword to all the international bowlers of his era. And from the time Richards first came up against Lillee, it was like two irresistible forces meeting toe-to-toe; a heavyweight fight between two unrelenting combatants. Their contests were always take-no-prisoners affairs. Lillee's well-documented battle to overcome near-crippling back injury and return from relative obscurity to dominate the Test arena provides adequate proof of the calibre of his fighting qualities. He did what it took to take you out, sometimes roughing you up along the way.

The young Lillee was once castigated by WA captain Tony Lock, who told him bluntly, 'Dennis, you are bowling like a Fucking Old Tart.' Teammate and later WA captain John Inverarity grabbed hold of Lock's description and coined Lillee's nickname, FOT.

In December 1971, Lillee blitzed a strong World XI batting line-up in Perth, taking 8/29, polishing off the Garry Sobers' led side with 6/0. He played World Series Cricket for a couple of years and during that time he worked diligently on his approach to the wicket and his delivery. If it were possible, he became an even better bowler in the technical sense. The famous 'caught Marsh bowled Lillee' dismissal appears on Test match scorecards 95 times. At the WACA Ground in Perth the Lillee–Marsh Stand was named in their honour. In 70 Tests, Lillee took 355 wickets at 23.92 with 23 hauls of five wickets. Lillee's best Test figures were 7/83 against the West Indies at the MCG in 1981.

But figures cannot tell of a bowler's strategy, the way a victim is stalked and finally put to the sword. Struggling with his body out there, as he often did over his stellar career, Lillee called upon all his inner reserves and often drove himself upward and onward by sheer willpower. He was instrumental in helping establish World Series Cricket and when he hung up his boots he became a splendid fast bowling coach, mentoring, among many others, Jason Gillespie, Brett Lee and Mitchell Johnson. For years Dennis ran the MRF Pace Foundation in Chennai, India, and was president of the Western Australian Cricket Association (WACA) for 11 years.

As the cricket gods blessed the game with the likes of Trumper, Bradman, Viv Richards, Wasim Akram, Keith Miller and Shane Warne, so too they have done the game proud by bringing D.K. Lillee onto the big stage for all to enjoy and admire. There was a poetry in his approach to the wicket, a perfect symmetry in his action and never-ending fire in his belly. Lillee had the heart of a lion and an inexhaustible will to succeed.

Chapter 19

The art of cricket

Cricket followers have revelled in the artistry of many great players, including Bradman, Trumper, Tendulker, Grimmett, O'Reilly and Warne. However, a select band of celebrated cricketers have turned their hand to art of another kind. Clarrie Grimmett was not only a wonderful exponent of leg-spin bowling, he was also a clever artist. While bowling was Clarrie's 'breath of life', this veritable Bradman of Spin could draw admirably with pencil or brush.

Long before he came to Australia Clarrie was an apprentice sign-writer in Wellington. Art seemed a natural progression for him and when he left the sign-writing trade, Clarrie, for a time, ran the Clarrie Grimmett Bag Shop in Adelaide. As women browsed, the little spin wizard surreptitiously sketched their profiles on the back of a brown-paper bag, a stack of which he kept within arm's reach under the bench top. Later, some of these sketches became works on canvas.

But Grimmett's art never became widely known, for he wanted to be taken seriously; not seen as some sort of comic turn, like he perceived Arthur Mailey, his arch rival in spin. After his career ended, Mailey bought a butcher's shop in Cronulla, a Sydney suburb. On his shop front window appeared the words: 'I used to bowl tripe; then I wrote it; now I sell it!'

Mailey was raised in Zetland, a slum suburb in Sydney, where he worked in a variety of labouring jobs before cricket and art, sketching in pen and ink and painting in oils, began to consume him. In 1921, the first of his two England tours with the Australian team, Mailey's sketches and cartoons so impressed the *London Bystander and Graphic* that the magazine offered him a job at the handsome salary of £20 a week.

Mailey spent his time away from cricket visiting galleries, museums and theatres, soaking up everything to do with British culture. One day he was at his easel at a house in an estate bordering the Royal House at Sandringham when none other a personage than King George V paid him a surprise visit. He took one look at Mailey's painting of an English summer's scene and the King's speech took on a critical tone: 'Your sun is out of shape.' Quick as a flash, Mailey returned fire: 'Your majesty, since arriving in England I had almost forgotten what the sun looks like.'

That wonderful English cricket writer Neville Cardus said of Mailey: '(He's) the most fascinating cricketer I have known' and 'an artist in every part of his nature'.

Mailey's pen-and-ink sketchbooks fetch good prices these days. A 15.5 x 10 cm Arthur Mailey cartoon entitled 'Australian Press Box' is now selling for £350. His autobiography *10 for 66 and all that* (reprinted in 2008) is a brilliant piece of writing and the added bonus is that the book contains a wealth of the Mailey sketches.

Grimmett and Mailey knew all there was about visualisation. Both were artists as spin bowlers; one, Mailey, bowled like the 'millionaire' and the other, Grimmett, bowled like the 'miser', but despite their differences in bowling strategy and attitude they both revelled in art. They could apply what they 'saw' in their mind's eye to their bowling or to the canvas.

In 1991 at Dunedin I was coaching 60 spinners and I decided to have the spinners use a large wall as target practice. There were 20 groups of three bowling at the wall from a distance of some 10 paces. Suddenly a man rushed towards us, waving his arms frantically. 'Stop, stop,' he bellowed, still waving his arms, his eyes ablaze. Turns out he was the curator of the Dunedin Art Gallery and we were bowling at the gallery wall. I never discovered how many paintings hit the floor that day.

While Grimmett's paintings are good and Mailey's cartoons and sketches a delight, a more famous artist by far is the former Gloucester and England wicketkeeper Jack Russell. He turned out for England 54 times but his enduring fame will undoubtedly stem from his gift as an impressionist and portrait painter.

Jack has painted the portraits of such luminaries as HRH Prince Philip, Duke of Edinburgh, singer Eric Clapton, comedian Norman Wisdom and footballer Bobby Charlton. His evocative painting *Cockleshell Heroes* hangs in the Royal Marines Barracks in Poole and other Russell works hang in such diverse places as the Bradman Museum in Bowral and the Tower of London. As a wicketkeeper, Jack was eccentric, ever wearing his favourite black gloves until they literally fell to pieces.

When rain stops play, as it did at New Road in the early 1980s, young Gloucester 'keeper Jack Russell didn't do as the others did, sit about playing cards or chatting. He went for a walk in to town. In Worcester he bought a sketch pad and pencils, then strolled back to the cricket along the banks of the Severn. He would later say, 'If Rembrandt could do it, so could I.'

Jack kept on keeping on in cricket and he continued to draw. On the England tour of Pakistan in 1987 Jack, the team's second keeper, played only two days of a six-week tour, so he had lots of spare time to take photographs and draw. Upon his return to England Jack displayed 40 sketches in a gallery in Bristol and they sold out in two days. Nowadays most of Jack's single paintings sell for £25,000 (or more); not bad for a young man who never studied art at school.

Recently I stayed overnight with Ian Redpath at his family home in Geelong. I was there to speak at the Redpath Society dinner and an hour or so before we left for the event I let slip that I had started painting in acrylic, confessing that if I made a mistake I could paint over and start again. The bearded Redpath smiled, raised a bushy eyebrow and nodded towards a framed painting hanging on his lounge-room wall. His impressive watercolour is of St Nicholas Church, Longparish, former long-term cricket correspondent of *The Times* and one of the Redpath family's dearest England-based friends, John Woodcock's place of worship. 'Wooders' dutifully makes the short walk from his home, The Old Curacy, to open up the church three times a week. He will be delighted to learn his church has been portrayed in this way, especially by the hand of his good Australian friend.

St Nicholas Church was built in the 13th century. Its latest acquisition is a stained-glass window commemorating one of Britain's most successful fighter pilots of World War One, Major Lanoe George Hawker. Major Hawker, VC, DSO, was killed over France in 1916 in a dogfight with German ace Manfred Von Richtofen, known as the Red Baron,.

Once a week Redders accompanies ex-Geelong footballer and Brownlow Medal winner Alastair Lord to a hall in the centre of the town of Geelong and the pair focus on their painting. Nowadays he also enjoys coaching cricket and is often seen working at the Geelong Cricket Club. Redders' days of running an antique dealership are now over. He still dabbles in renovating the odd piece of furniture in his home work shed, but painting, his hobby for the past eight years, has become a joy. Many ex-players find their niche in writing or broadcasting; some, like Ian Redpath, paint.

Portraits of cricketers past and present is my goal, my first portrait an acrylic study of Victor Trumper, the greatest batsman of cricket's Golden Age (1894–1914).

Perhaps there is also an art in a cricketer picking the right pathway in life after their playing days are over.

Chapter 20

Viv Richards: Master Blaster

No batsman in Test match history intimidated bowlers quite so dramatically as the West Indian 'Master Blaster', Viv Richards. Youngsters are encouraged to cross with the departing batsmen on the field of play as the outgoing batsman wends his way back to the pavilion. Not Viv. The cricket field was his stage and Viv liked to keep the opposition, especially the bowlers, waiting.

There was an air of great anticipation at the ground when Viv Richards sauntered to the middle. He held his bat in his right hand and swung it in a windmill action as if it was a war club and Viv was off to battle. As he moved closer to the centre the crowd cheered and the bowlers felt a chill running down their spine. His West Indian Test cap was worn at a tilt exuding a belief and a confidence one might identify with the greatest of prize fighters, Muhammad Ali.

When in the mood Viv toyed with bowlers. When he grew bored by the lack of challenge, he proceeded to belt the hell out them. Viv had all the shots – off and cover drives, his famous shuffle to the off-side to be in the perfect position to smack the ball wide of mid-on, deft cuts and savage pulls and hooks. The Master Blaster in full cry was a batsman who simply tore an attack to shreds. He took no prisoners.

Picture the scene. Viv holding his head high and sporting what is commonly known as a Roman nose, aquiline with a high bridge and a hook. He strolls to the crease – half saunter, half swagger – his jaw working overtime chewing gum. There is an air of disdain, a sense of seeming disinterest about him. He appears so relaxed he could be looking for a place to lie down. But no, Richards is on a mission. He takes guard: the look-a-like Churchill victory sign tells us he is batting on middle and leg. Pity the bowler who strays to leg. He looks about the field, noting the gaps and just who is fielding where. He keeps it simple, running it through his mind: 'There's a single here and single there ... oh, what the matter, it's a four or six.' He saunters down the wicket and taps the turf with the toe of his Slazenger bat, never taking his eye off the bowler. Viv's mind chews over the possibilities even as the bowler is about to release the ball. Dennis Lillee steams in: it is the clash of the Titans. Lillee's first ball is a quick outswinger on a line just outside off, a perfect line and length to most batsmen. Not Viv. The West Indian shuffles to a spot outside off and spanks the ball with the velocity of a tracer bullet past mid to the boundary.

Viv's menacing manner at the crease was the stuff of legend: magnificent theatre. He was the game's most ferocious hooker in his time and probably of all time. Jeff Thomson, arguably the fastest bowler to draw breath, got the ball to scream off a length at the batsman's throat. He was lethal. No one could hook Thommo. No one, that is, except Viv Richards. Even Thommo copped it sweet from the Master Blaster's bat: usually a resounding thwack which had the ball scream over square leg like a jet taking off at supersonic speed.

All the same Viv was wary of Thommo. He said of the fast bowler: 'When Thommo found that right length, the length that allowed him to gain amazing bounce – he was as good as it gets. The number of wickets he took with balls lifting sharply off a good length was amazing. For that special delivery, no one could match Jeff Thomson for raw, lethal pace.'

In the third Test of the 1975–76 series at the MCG, Thommo got his special ball to lift dramatically off a length and Lawrence Rowe was good enough to edge it. The ball hurtled towards first slip and there Ian Chappell took it in both hands as he turned his body to his left side. The brute of a ball ended in a wonderful catch, probably the best I've seen at first slip from Chappelli.

Viv didn't set the world on fire in Australia that series. For a few Tests he hardly bothered the scorers. His big scores in the final two Tests were modest by the standards he was soon to set, a mere prelude to his super England summer of 1976. That calendar year Richards scored a remarkable 1710 Test runs, including 829 in the series against England, despite missing one Test match. Viv hit two double hundreds that series, including a brilliant 291 at The Oval helping the West Indies to trounce the home side 3-nil.

Richards' swagger and his presence at the crease intimidated and unnerved the best bowlers of his time. Statistically he is among many batsmen who have averaged 50 in a career of more than 30 Tests, however the manner in which Viv destroyed entire attacks — one bowler after the other — placed him at the highest level of batsmen. In 121 Test matches Viv scored 8350 runs with 24 centuries at an average of 50.23. In 14 World Series Cricket Supertests for the West Indies Viv hit 1281 runs at 58.23 with four centuries. He scored 7000 ODI runs at a rate of 92 runs per 100 balls. He averaged 47 in those matches.

When it came to batting against the best of bowling, he was as sure of himself and as carefree as a kid let loose in a lolly shop. I never saw Viv go to bat wearing a helmet. There was always his maroon Windies Cap, which he wore that day at the SCG in the summer of 1975–76 when he was hit on the forehead. Greg Chappell was bowling his gentle medium pacers and the ball rose unexpectedly from a length and hit Viv squarely on the forehead. Viv didn't rub the affected area, he merely shook his head, made a slight adjustment to his maroon cap and faced up for the next ball.

Viv Richards took over from Clive Lloyd as Windies captain and led the Calypso kings in 50 Tests, winning 27 and losing just eight during an era which saw the Windies totally dominate world cricket. The Windies' pace barrage was awesome. These men — Andy Roberts, Michael Holding, Joel Garner, Malcolm Marshall, Curtly Ambrose and a host of others — became legends. First Lloyd, then Viv, maintained a four-pronged pace attack which proved relentlessly persistent and highly successful.

Then there was the batting power of Gordon Greenidge and Desmond Haynes at the top of the order, Viv, Lloyd, Lawrence Rowe, Alvin Kalicharran and Jeffrey Dugon, the 'keeper, who had the ability to peel off centuries.

Their fielding was magnificent. Lloyd at slip and Viv lurking at point or extra cover, swift over the ground. Possessing strong, safe hands he swooped on the ball in one swift action and he had a deadly accurate throw. Richards ran out a number of key Australian batsmen in the first World Cup at Lord's in 1975, helping the West Indies to historic victory, prompting Doug Walters to say: 'There are no live rabbits in Antigua (Viv's home town).'

Viv played the game hard but fair and he could not abide sledging. In 1980, during a Test match at Adelaide Oval, Australian paceman Len Pascoe decided to put Viv to the sword first ball of his over. Lennie thought that if he were to run through the crease and bowl a big no ball on purpose, it would get Viv on the back foot and unsettle him. Pascoe approached from the scoreboard end and sure enough he ran way past the bowling crease, at least two paces, and the ball made Viv duck and weave as it whistled past his eyes.

Viv was furious and he hammered the handle of his bat angrily while he swaggered down the pitch to about the halfway mark, tapped the turf with the toe of his bat, eyeballed Pascoe who was saying enough for Umpire Max O'Connell to intervene, and gave the Australian fast bowler the V sign. Viv said to O'Connell: 'Don't worry about me, man. Watch what happens to this next ball.'

Pascoe's master plan was to have Viv on the back foot first ball, which he succeeded in making happen, then bowl the champion with a searing yorker. Viv was waiting. Sure enough, along came the Pascoe attempted yorker and Viv smacked the ball with his Slazenger bat with such ferocious power that Pascoe was almost decapitated as the ball flew close to his head on the way to the fence on what was then a incredibly long straight boundary at Adelaide Oval. Viv didn't move from the crease. He stood eyeballing Pascoe, all the time hammering the top of the handle of his bat with his gloved right fist. He didn't say a word, just stood there chewing his gum. Lennie walked back to his mark like a man who had just fallen from grace in the eyes of the cricket world.

That was some counter-measure from Viv Richards; quite the best 'sledge' I'd seen on the Test stage, and not an expletive in sight.

Viv Richards was notorious for punishing bowlers who dared sledge him. Opening bowler Greg Thomas was growing frustrated on a day Viv was playing for Somerset against Glamorgan,. He had Viv playing and missing balls outside the off stump three times in a row. Thomas stood in front of Viv and said sarcastically: 'It's red, it's round and it weighs about five ounces; in case you were wondering.'

Viv shook his head, laughed and settled down over his bat. The next Thomas delivery was a juicy half volley, which Richards smashed right out of the ground, the ball landing in the river outside the ground. Viv found himself a metre from Thomas. He eyeballed him and with a slight grin said: 'You know what it looks like, Greg. Now go and find it!'

In the year 2000, Viv Richards was named as one of the five *Wisden Almanack*'s best cricketers of the century.

Sometimes, as I once discovered when playing for South Australia against the West Indies on the Adelaide Oval in 1979-80, Viv would block every ball of an over. Each ball perfectly covered by a defence as stout as any the world has seen. If there was the semblance of a gap twixt bat and pad, perhaps only something as infinitesimal as a dwarf flea could pass through Maybe Viv was resting, for the next over he hit out at anything and everything and continued doing so for the rest of his innings.

Because of his swagger some people perceived Viv to be arrogant. Dr Donald Beard, the long-time South Australian Cricket Association doctor, got to know numerous West Indian cricketers, inviting many to his home for dinner whenever they were in town.

> Sir Vivian Richards – Viv Richards – was, of course, a wonderful batsman, possessing an array of glorious strokes that I can still recall, but people thought he was a bit stand-offish and didn't mix freely. I got to know him. He had an injury one day and I drove him to hospital for X-rays. We talked a bit about his cricketing life.
>
> It came out how much he loved cricket and how much he loved boys who played cricket and what he did for them. He did a tremendous amount coaching young boys both in the West Indies and England.
>
> He talked about this in a most sincere manner. He opened up and I was

fortunate to have the chance to talk to him in this way. I saw the other side of Richards, the humble, caring side. In his photograph he looks supercilious, looking slightly upwards as if the rest of the world didn't matter. I think that was, partly, shyness. There was a long-held opinion that Viv was arrogant. He was much like (Don) Bradman – many people thought he was a bit arrogant. There is no way Richards is arrogant. He loves cricket and he loves people.

In 1983 and 1984, Viv Richards refused to sign a blank cheque to play for a rebel West Indian cricket team that toured South Africa. The republic was then still held in the racist grip of apartheid. Sir Vivian Richards: what a cricketer; what a man.

Chapter 21

'Fiery Fred' Trueman

Fred Trueman was arguably England's finest fast bowler. A stocky, barrel-chested man, Fred bowled his heart out for Yorkshire and England. Born Frederick Sewards Trueman at Stainton (North Yorkshire) on 6 February 1931, the fourth of Dick and Ethel Trueman's seven children, Fred's early education was at the village school in Stainton. Legend has it he was born during a snowstorm in the outside toilet close to the pit yard and had to sleep in a drawer pulled from the sideboard. Fred's upbringing was very loving, but poor and hard. His father, later joined by his brother, worked at the Maltby Main Colliery. It was hard, unforgiving and dirty work. The men toiled all week for a pittance, their only luxury pints of bitter at the local after work. Encouraged by Dick Trueman, a father who wanted something better for his son than work as a miner, Fred began bowling a cricket ball when he was four years old. At Maltby Secondary School Fred's real cricket education began. Two teachers at the school – Dickie Harrison and Tommy Stubbs – recognised young Fred's ability and picked him for the school team. Fred always acknowledged one of his early coaches, Cyril Turner, who taught him to 'hold the ball properly' and showed him the correct seam position for the out swinger and the in swinger. Fred learnt to swing the ball both ways at genuine pace and it was Turner who impressed upon him the importance of a smooth follow through and the importance of 'completing your action'. He swiftly came through the ranks at Yorkshire and in the winter of 1947-48

Fred received an invitation to attend indoor coaching classes at Headingly, Leeds, under the supervision of Bill Bowes and Arthur Mitchell.

The following summer Fred met other Yorkshire luminaries including Brian Close and Ray Illingworth. A successful season with the Yorkshire Federation team for players under 18 attracted praise from none other than ex-Yorkshire and England champions George Hirst and Herbert Sutcliffe, who wrote in a local newspaper that Fred Trueman would soon be playing for Yorkshire. Within a year he was in the Yorkshire team and he went on to play first-class cricket from 1949–1969, taking 2304 wickets at an average of 18.29. In 67 Test matches he took 307 wickets at 21.57, statistically brilliant, but Fred was above mere stats. Fiercely competitive from the first ball to last, when stumps were drawn Fred would light up his favourite pipe and get stuck into a pint of bitter.

Fred Trueman possessed a stocky body of enormous strength: the bottom of a shire-horse, billiard table carved legs and forearms, a barrel chest and that familiar thick mop of Brylcreem ® slicked-black hair, which flopped about crazily as he moved in to bowl.

It is now more than 50 years since Trueman played his last Test match, against New Zealand at Lord's. Britain was changing. The Beatles were awarded MBEs that year and British Rail had taken up the 24-hour clock. Fred's long cotton sleeves still tumbled down over those imposing forearms, but his genuine pace was no more. A correspondent for the *Guardian* even went do far as to call Fred 'an honest plodder'. Such a description was sacrilege for the proud Yorkshireman whose classic side-on action and amazing stamina had served Yorkshire and England so well for more years than the locusts have eaten.

Fred had a brilliant sense of humour, albeit rather ribald. He was naughtiness personified. He became a terrific storyteller, appearing at myriad dinners to give hilarious after-dinner speeches. Once he was asked, along with two others I will call Lady Bridge and Lord Carrington, 'Your idea of a gentleman'. Mind you, this was live television, with an estimated audience of three million. Lady Bridge was first to bat: 'My idea of a gentleman is someone who allows me into a lift first or opens the car door for me.'

'Ah, Lord Carrington,' said the TV host, 'And your idea?'

'Well, my idea of a gentlemen is someone who lights his cigarette first with a match and milady's first with a lighter.'

Fred was next. There was a long pause. 'My idea of a gentleman is someone who gets out of the bath to have a piss!'

There were no airs and graces about Fred. He told it as it was and he was never afraid to say what he thought. After his cricket career ended a celebrity asked him on television, 'What do you want to call your autobiography?'

'I should call it "The definitive volume on the finest fast bowler that ever drew breath".'

To play for Yorkshire in the 1950s and 1960s was special as you became a member of a tightly knit band of brothers. In those days Yorkshire County Cricket Club's constitution stipulated that only those born within the county boundary were eligible to play for Yorkshire.

Until 1963 there were professionals (those who were paid to play) and amateurs (usually people who were brought up by a well-off family). Extraordinarily the amateurs came on to the ground through a different gate than the professionals. By 1965 Yorkshire cricket stretched its way across the whole expanse of Yorkshire. The club played at seven scattered grounds: Bradford, Harrogate, Hull, Middlesborough, Scarborough and Sheffield. In those days it was tough to become a member. Yorkshire and its cricketers were revered. Fred always loved walking out on to the field with his ten teammates, all proudly wearing the famous white rose cap. Trueman was in his element: Fiery Fred, fast, charismatic, caustic and charming. James Greenfield, sports editor of the *Yorkshire Post* for many years, remembers a man who would have done anything for his club.

> Fred once said that he would crawl through broken glass to play for Yorkshire. And that's true. These days once players are picked for England they don't play so much for their county.
>
> Fred was a talismanic figure, prepared to sacrifice himself, and he did stand out even in the great Yorkshire team of those days. [Frank] Tyson was faster but Trueman had longevity. He also had a very good physique. I remember Yorkshire had a lady physio and she said God only gave out one perfect physique and she gave it to Fred Trueman.

For years Fred and Geoff Boycott were at loggerheads, both as Yorkshire stubborn as the other, but soon enough before Fred died the pair shook hands and made up for all those years of ill feeling.

Fred's talent, skill and popularity were such that British Prime Minister Harold Wilson once described him as the 'greatest living Yorkshireman'. Even so, Trueman was omitted from numerous England teams because he was frequently in conflict with the cricket establishment, which he often criticised for its perceived 'snobbishness' and hypocrisy. Legend has it that at a reception in the West Indies Fred made a pass at an elegant woman and she said: 'As a woman I am very flattered Mr Trueman, but as the Governor's wife I am absolutely outraged!' On that same tour Fred was at another formal dinner when he was said to have ordered a local dignitary, apparently the Indian High Commissioner, to 'Pass t'salt, Gunga Din.'

Fred Trueman was a fabulous fast bowler with a great, rhythmical approach, high front arm and a classical side-on action. I once asked Sir Donald Bradman if there were any bowlers he would liked to have faced. Smiling he replied, 'Plenty.'

I rephrased my question: 'Sir Donald, I meant any particular bowlers who would have provided you with a real challenge.'

'Yes, I'll name one – Fred Trueman. I thought he was a wonderful bowler, beautiful rhythm, classic action and a late moving out-swinger drawing the batsman into playing a ball he didn't want to play.'

People loved Fred's comments on the BBC as a radio commentator and providing expert summaries of matches. He worked for years on *Test Match Special* and was a favourite of John Arlott's, both as a cricketer and a man. Fred was awarded the OBE, for services to cricket, in the 1989 Queen's Birthday honours list.

In the 1970s Trueman anchored a Yorkshire Television ITV program, *Indoor League*. The show was notable for a clear focus on the Northern working class . There was Fred smoking his pipe and holding a pint of bitter overseeing such pub games as darts, billiards, shove ha'penny, skittles and arm wrestling. He even made a guest appearance in an episode of *Dad's Army* and for 43 years he wrote a column in *Sunday People*, providing coverage of cricket and rugby league.

'FIERY FRED' TRUEMAN

On the night of 19 August 1975, the abandoned last day of the Headingly, Leeds, third Test, I spoke to a fuming Trueman. Fred was angry on two counts. One, the match was cruelly cut short on the last day because vandals had snuck under the covers overnight and damaged the wicket. They sabotaged the game by cutting holes with knives in an area near the popping crease and they poured a gallon of crude oil in the region where a good length would have pitched. Further Fred was livid over the sentence handed down to the six members of the IRA convicted of having carried out the Birmingham bombings. On 21 November 1974 bombs exploded in two public houses, killing 21 people and injuring 182 others.

My question: 'If you were presiding over the case, what would you, Judge Fred Trueman, have done with these six bombers?'

'Well, Rowdy. Firstly I have to take you back to 1972,' Fred mused. 'It was the time of the 1972 Leeds fourth Test match. At that very ground Keith Fletcher got a duck, but worse still ... he dropped everything which came his way at first slip.'

Fletcher, the Essex and England batsman, the man they called the 'Gnome', didn't fare too well in the game just completed in August 1975. He scored 8 and 14 and, yes, he dropped a couple of easy chances.

Fred then paused. Taking a sip of his pint he raised his eyebrows, which could never have hidden the mischievous glint in his eye.

'Now, you ask me what I'd do with those bombers. I'd take 'em up top of grandstand and push 'em off one by one and have bloody Keith Fletcher, down below at grass level, to try and catch 'em!'

Fred, aged 75, died in 2006 and was interred in Bolton Abbey: forever at rest in his beloved Yorkshire.

Chapter 22

Tibby Cotter's last charge

Minutes after the famous cavalry charge, stretcher-bearer 924, Trooper Albert 'Tibby' Cotter, lay dead.

That day, Wednesday 31 October 1917, was significant in the world of cricket, for Tibby Cotter was the lone Australian Test cricketer to be killed in WWI.

After riding into battle with the 12th Australian Light Horse against a heavily armed and dug-in Turkish brigade, Trooper Cotter found hundreds of dead soldiers lying in the choking dust of the Sinai. Amid the confusion Trooper Cotter noticed a Turkish field gun, with its detachment of horses and men, making a hasty retreat towards Beersheeba. As he neared the escaping enemy, the unarmed trooper sighed relief as the Turks threw down their weapons in a seeming gesture of surrender. He lent over in his saddle to grab the lead horse and one of the Turks produced a pistol and shot Trooper Cotter in the back of the head. Just 27 days earlier his older brother Private John Cotter was killed at Ypres in Belgium. A total of 494 first-class cricketers worldwide were killed during the Great War, among them many Australians, however, only one of them, Cotter, was an Australian Test player. The Jeff Thomson of his day, Cotter bowled at typhoon velocity, delighting all and sundry by consistently breaking the stumps when he clean bowled a batsman. From 1904–1912 he played 21 Tests, taking 89 wickets at 28.94 with seven hauls of five wickets in an innings.

He was also no mug with the bat. In a grade game for Glebe in Sydney Cotter smashed 16 sixes in scoring 152 in 70 minutes. Cotter toured England in 1905 and 1909 and on one occasion hit W.G. Grace in the breadbasket with a wild beam ball. Cotter joined the AIF in April 1915, aged 31. An ex-Test cricketer joining up was a coup for the recruiting team. Despite having no riding ability, Cotter was accepted into the 1st Australian Light Horse and was commended for displaying great courage and 'fine work under heavy fire'. On 17 December 1915 he played cricket with fellow troops on the Gallipoli Peninsula. The game was a ruse to distract the Turks while Allied troops began to depart from the battlefield. After Gallipoli, Trooper Cotter transferred to the 12th Light Horse.

Cotter was among the Big Six famous players who in 1912 rebelled over the Australian Cricket Board's conditions for the tour of England. Along with Victor Trumper, Clem Hill, Warwick Armstrong, Vernon Ransford and Hanson Carter, Cotter objected to the Board appointing the manager of their choice. The players wanted to appoint their own man, Frank Laver. The players were adamant, no Laver as manager and they would not tour. None of the Big Six toured England in 1912. Their war of words with the Board began an era characterised by the administrators' petty and absurd attitude towards the players, which only began to change with the World Series Cricket revolution.

Cotter was cast as something of a larrikin. He was cricket's first 'modern fast bowler' in that he never worried about accuracy. Cotter was the first pace bowler to intimidate batsmen with the bouncer and operate with a slips cordon. In February 2015 the Tibby Cotter walkway was opened at Anzac Parade linking Moore Park to the SCG. So long after the silence of the guns we remember the fallen.

Ernest Hemingway probably said it best: 'World War I was the most colossal, murderous, mismanaged butchery that has ever taken place on earth. Any writer who said otherwise lied, so the writers either wrote propaganda, shut up, or fought.'

Chapter 23

Ian Michael Chappell: our best Test captain

Ian Chappell was Australia's greatest Test match captain. Great leaders are born, not made, because the best of them are intuitive, follow their instincts, have great belief in themselves and are both friend and mentor to their charges.

Chappelli had all those attributes and some. He became the Australian captain on Thursday 4 February 1971. As was his habit at lunchtime, away from his duties as a W.D. & H.O. Wills salesman, Ian had ducked into Adelaide's Overway Hotel for a schnitzel and beer when the barman called him to the phone.

'Congratulations, Chappelli, well done,' Allan Shiell, cricket writer for the afternoon daily, the *News*, called down the line. 'You are now the Australian Test captain.' The pair spoke for a while, then Ian sipped his beer before reaching for his wallet again, this time to retrieve a crumpled piece of paper. He looked at the handwritten words: 'My ambition is to captain Australia.'

In 1959, when Ian was sixteen, he was selected to play in the South Australian State Schoolboys' Team of the Year. His reward for being picked was two days' coaching at the Adelaide Oval from then State coach, former SA and Test fast bowler Geff Noblet. Chappelli was disappointed that the squad didn't get the chance to bat against some of the State's best bowlers in the nets. 'That would have given us all a good indication of how much we needed to improve, how much work we needed to do to get to A grade district level.'

To captain Australia was undoubtedly his ambition, but Chappelli didn't expect to get the job, especially in the wake of a conversation over a few beers in a Kent pub back in 1968. We were on the Australian tour of England and a few of us were at the bar when our manager Bob Parish suddenly blurted: 'Ian, if you don't curb your swearing you'll never captain Australia.' Chappelli was amazed on two counts: firstly, that Bob Parish who rarely walked into a bar was present and, secondly, because 'I'd never considered myself a candidate for the job.' Long after Chappell had retired from cricket he was playing a round of golf at the Pennant Hills Golf Club in Sydney with former teammates Graeme Watson and Brian Taber. Making up the golfing four was Neil Harvey, a Test selector during Chappell's captaincy tenure. Watson and Taber left the club. Chappell was left enjoying a drink with Harvey and he grabbed the chance to talk one-on-one with the old champion. 'Just which one of the three selectors wanted me to captain the Test team?'

'Me, bloody me,' was Harvey's typical matter-of-fact reply.

It gave Chappelli an opportunity to thank the man who lobbied so hard to get him the role. In the summer of 1958–59 Harvey, a great player, was expected to get the Test captaincy when Ian Craig retired through illness. Richie Benaud got the job and Harvey became his loyal and supportive deputy. When Benaud pulled out of the second Test against England at Lord's in 1961, Harvey led the side for the first and only time. Australia won the match, thanks to a brave innings of 130 by Bill Lawry and Graham Mckenzie's brilliant debut with the ball. Neil Harvey needed to persuade at least one of his fellow selectors, either Sir Donald Bradman or Sam Loxton, that Ian Chappell was the right person to take over from Bill Lawry as Test captain.

Reading between the lines I reckon Harvey got his way – getting Ian Chappell the Test captaincy – by convincing his good friend Sam Loxton to join him in outvoting Bradman. In the wake of the Ian Chappell appointment, Sir Donald Bradman resigned from the Test selection panel. As soon as he learnt he had the captaincy, Chappelli sat down and listed all the qualities of leadership that he liked in the captains he had played under, Les Favell (SA), Bob Simpson and Bill Lawry (Australia). Then he listed the things he disliked about their captaincy and he made a mental note to avoid those traps.

Leading up to Chappell's appointment, Australia had undertaken an exhausting seven-month tour of Ceylon (Sri Lanka), India and South Africa. In those days Ceylon did not play Test cricket, so there were just a few first-class games, one an unofficial Test which ended in a draw. Chappelli batted brilliantly in India to help Australia win the series 3–1. But it was a gruelling tour. The players were accommodated in dreadful hovels of hotels, the food was terrible and the team was indeed lucky to have won so convincingly.

South Africa was very different. Midway through the tour the South African Cricket Association suggested that a fifth Test should be played, an extra one to the four scheduled matches. The South Africans obviously wanted to swell their coffers; the extra Test was to be played in Johannesburg, where a full house at the Wanderers Ground was certain. The home team had won the first two Tests. At a team meeting Fred Bennett (Manager) and Bill Lawry explained to the team that the South African proposal had been agreed to by the Australian Cricket Board of Control for International Cricket. The last two meaningless first class games (against West Province and Orange Free State) would be scrapped and the fifth Test played in their stead. Ian Chappell could not have been less impressed.

'We've been sold down the river by the Board. First they send us here after India. As your vice captain I say that this is a great opportunity, one not to be missed. Look, you guys, we have the bastards (the Board) over a barrel.'

To play the fifth Test match the players were asked to sign a new contract because the tour would have then gone on three days longer than the period they had signed up for in the first place. The Board was going to pay each player an additional $200 if they agreed to play a fifth Test. When the Australians asked for an extra $300, making it $500, the Board refused. The Wanderers Club offered to make up the extra $300.

'One player said he could use the money and they should go ahead and play the match with the dissenters.' Ian Chappell took out his chequebook and banged it on the table.

'Look, he said, 'if you want the money so badly I'll write out a cheque for you now. We've got this opportunity to stand up and be counted and we'll fucking well tell them that we are not playing. Look at the fucking itinerary they've given us – India then South Africa. Then Bill Lawry stepped in and said, "Righto, it's either all-in or all-out. It's obvious that some of you don't want to play, so it's all over, forget it."' The fifth Test was never played because Lawry would have only accepted a unanimous decision.

Chappelli's strong leadership at that meeting unquestionably influenced many of the players. But the Board didn't like it one iota. Undoubtedly a big black mark was struck against Bill Lawry's name. With the Board hovering over him like an ogre with a razor-sharp axe, Lawry needed runs and plenty of them to retain his place in the coming Ashes series against Ray Illingworth's England team in the summer of 1970–71. Runs again eluded Lawry and he was dumped after the drawn Test in Adelaide when Illingworth inexplicably opted not to enforce the follow on.

Ian Chappell (104) and Keith Stackpole (136) saved Australia's bacon. For the Seventh – and final – Test match at the SCG, the selectors dropped Lawry along with spinners John Gleeson, Ashley Mallett and Alan 'Froggy' Thompson. In came Victoria's left-hand opening bat, Ken Eastwood, and leg-spinners Terry Jenner (SA) and Kerry O'Keeffe (NSW).

The Australians lost a closely fought final Test match and Illingworth's team won the Ashes. Ian Chappell led the side well in a losing battle. Then came the defining 1972 Australian Cricket team's tour of England. Chappelli reckoned that a Test win was so important to team morale and Australian cricket fans that the side was almost beside itself when England limped home in the first Test at Manchester.

The Waldorf Hotel was our home base and some among the team – Ian Chappell, Doug Walters, Brian Taber, Graeme Watson, Dave Colley et al. – frequented the hotel's front bar in the Aldwych, which was just a Keith Miller drive from Australia House. One late afternoon after a long training session at Lord's, in walked Australia's latest fast bowling sensation Dennis Lillee, accompanied by his latest English fan, cricket tragic and music legend Mick Jagger. Mick loved fast bowling and he enjoyed watching Lillee, the latest and fastest firebrand bowler of the time.

Chappelli had his captain's allowance and he always insisted on buying the next round. It was hard for anyone else to buy a beer. Another celebrity regular to the Waldorf Hotel front bar was Ed Devereaux, best known in Australia for his role in *Skippy, the Bush Kangaroo*. An admirer of Chappell, Devereaux said: 'Ian reminds me of Paul Newman; he has presence. The guy walks into a room and everyone looks up. You either have that sort of charisma or you don't.'

Chappelli jealously guarded his right to relax in the bar and refused to sign autographs there. He would say, 'Look, mate, this place is our home away from home. It is our lounge-room, if you like. Now you wouldn't barge into my lounge-room demanding autographs, so don't do it here.'

There was a fabulous camaraderie among the players on tour. On the team coach there was always music blaring: Don McLean's immortal 'American Pie'; Johnny Nash's 'I Can See Clearly Now'; Helen Reddy's 'I am Woman'; Bill Thorpe's 'Most People I Know Think that I'm Crazy' and John Lennon's 'Imagine' were team favourites. There must have been a couple of numbers by the Rolling Stones. Some way, somehow, a recording studio wanted to make a record; incredibly two separate numbers of a 45 rpm sung by the 1972 Australian Cricket Team. We attended a boxing match-cum-black-tie dinner in London until midnight, then armed with a case or two of bottled beer we found ourselves in a dingy studio somewhere near Marble Arch. We sang our little hearts out for hours – the beer settled hoarse throats – until we cut two songs, 'Here Come the Aussies' and 'Bowl a ball, swing a bat'. Produced by Penny Farthing Records, a perfect name for that production company for none of us received one cent for our efforts.

'Here Come the Aussies' was top of the charts in Perth for a week or two, although we never thought our team would outdo the Stones or anyone else for that matter. You can still hear both songs through the magic of YouTube.

Chappelli got his wish for a Test match win at Lord's. Known as Massie's match (Bob Massie took 16/137 for the game, his Test match debut), England was bemused and befuddled by Massie's late swing. He got the ball to swing late both ways. After the England batting debacle, Ray Illingworth ordered his team to a room to watch highlights of the game and each wicket that had fallen to Massie. Trouble was the projector or the film or both were out of kilter. There was vision of the right-handed Massie bowling left-handed and the left-handed John Edrich batting right-handed.

Within a few minutes the Yorkshire in Illy (Ray Illingworth) shone. He threw up his hands and said: 'Right, lads, forget it all. Let's go and have a pint.' The series proved brilliant, perhaps the best Ashes series of them all until the 2005 rubber. Moreover it established Chappelli as an astute leader on and off the field.

He led Australia in 30 Tests for 15 wins and just five losses. Chappell never lost a series as captain. His last Test as captain was at the Oval in 1975. He handed the baton of leadership to brother Greg in Brisbane in 1975-76; a series in which Australia, under his brother, beat the West Indies 5-1. There have been other captains with a statistically more impressive record of wins and losses (Steve Waugh and Ricky Ponting come to mind), but to me Chappelli stands above them all, even his mentor Richie Benaud.

When World Series Cricket was announced in 1977, Chappell was summoned to the Park Street, Sydney, office of Kerry Packer. 'You are the WSC Australian captain,' Packer said.

When Chappelli protested saying he had handed the reins to his brother Greg, Packer slapped him on the back and bellowed, 'What do you think this is, son, a fucking democracy?'

Playing under Chappelli for South Australia was special. He empowered players. There was rarely a time when he stood before his men and dressed them down in the wake of a poor session in the field. He treated everyone equally, or almost everyone.

There was an occasion when things went slightly awry at the Gabba in Brisbane. As the SA team left the Gabba change-rooms for an afternoon in the field, Chappelli noticed our opening bowler Andrew Sincock blow drying his hair (long hair, a sort of poor man's Rod Stewart do) by the front door of the dressing-room as the players filed past.

We got onto the arena and Chappelli said: 'Rowd, you are opening the bowling.'

'Why?'

'Mate, no bloke who blow dries his fucking hair at the door of the dressing-room will ever open the bowling for any team I lead. You are bowling the other end to Fang (Wayne Prior).'

Ian Michael Chappell is honest as the day and is never hesitant to say it as it is in any circumstance, in any company. When a fellow cricketer falls on hard times, Chappelli is there for him. In a way, Chappelli is our captain for life.

Jack Hobbs, England's greatest opening batsman. [Courtesy R.L. Cardwell collection]

Victor Trumper, Australia's greatest batsman before Don Bradman. [Courtesy R.L. Cardwell collection]

English cricketers on a visit to a Bendigo gold mine.
From left: Fred Riches, Jack Hobbs, Hardstaff, Joe Humphries, Dick Young, and the manager of the mine.

W.G. Grace (centre, with striped cap and beard) led the annual Gentlemen versus Players match at Lord's in 1894. [Courtesy R.L. Cardwell collection]

A murky day for the Australians at Lord's, 1926. Front, from left. Sir Pelham 'Plum' Warner, Herbie Collins (Captain), Lord Hawke (MCC President) and Bill Woodfull. Jack Ryder, far right, rear. [Ashley Mallett collection]

Clarrie Grimmett in full flight.

Bill O'Reilly, the 'Tiger'.
[Ashley Mallett collection]

Frank Laver, Clem Hill, Albert Hopkins and Victor Trumper in mufti splendour in front of the Queen's Family Hotel, England, 1899. [Courtesy R.L. Cardwell collection]

Victor Trumper, Bradman's predecessor.

Don Bradman and Sid Barnes walk off the SCG in the 2nd Ashes Test of 1946/47. They scored a record 405 runs for the third wicket. Both men were out on 234.
[Courtesy R.L. Cardwell collection]

Clarrie Grimmett spins one up at Lord's practice at the start of Australia's 1930 tour.
[Ashley Mallett collection]

Finger flick mystery spinner John 'CHO' Gleeson in action.
[Courtesy R.L. Cardwell collection]

England firebrand and pipe enthusiast Freddie Trueman (at front) leads cigarette-smoking Trevor 'Barnacle' Bailey from training at the SCG in the summer of 1958/59.
[Courtesy R.L. Cardwell collection]

Gleeson agonises at South African all-rounder Eddie 'Bunter' Barlow's French cut. The look on the face of 'keeper Brian Taber says it all. It was a key moment in the Fourth Test v South Africa in Port Elizabeth. [Ashley Mallett collection]

Norm O'Neill and Bill Lawry coming out to open for Australia. Sydney Cricket Ground, 1964.

*Chappelli on the charge.
[Courtesy R.L. Cardwell
collection]*

*Elegant Greg Chappell cover drives in
classic style.
[Courtesy R.L. Cardwell collection]*

Lillee: 'Hey, Fletch ... a yorker? Or straight for your throat!'
[Courtesy R.L. Cardwell collection]

'FOT' in full flight. Dennis Lillee on the hunt.
[Courtesy R.L. Cardwell collection]

Champion New Zealand batsman Martin Crowe punches down the ground during a NZ v South Australia international at Adelaide Oval. SA's star recruit that summer, Martin's younger brother Jeff, is waiting for a snick at second slip.
[Courtesy R.L. Cardwell collection]

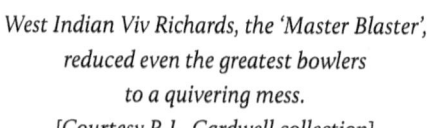

West Indian Viv Richards, the 'Master Blaster', reduced even the greatest bowlers to a quivering mess.
[Courtesy R.L. Cardwell collection]

Indian wizard, Erapally Prasanna, the greatest off-spinner the world has seen.
[Courtesy R.L. Cardwell collection]

Shane Warne, leg-spinner and Australia's leading wicket taker.
[Courtesy R.L. Cardwell collection]

West Australian State Schoolboys' team, National Carnival, Perth, 1959.
Front row: Far left, Tony Mann, third from left, Ashley Mallett (WA vice captain).
[Ashley Mallett collection]

A motley crew. Nedlands Baseball Club's Under-16 premiership team in the WA Baseball League, 1958.
Top row, far left: Baseball legend and International cricketer Charlie Puckett (coach).
Top row, fifth from left, Nick Mallett, author's brother. Front Row, far right: Ashley Mallett. [Ashley Mallett collection]

Ashley Mallett snares England opener David 'Bumble' Lloyd caught and bowled, Third Ashes Test, MCG, 1974/75.
[Ashley Mallett collection]

Ashley Mallett bowls the 'hope of the side' Len Pascoe to complete a stunning victory over NSW at the Adelaide Oval in 1980/81.
From left: Rick Darling, John Inverarity, Pascoe, and Trevor Robertson. Mallett is running towards the camera. [Ashley Mallett collection]

Bill Lawry's 1968 Australian team in England were presented with new ties and scarves at Tootal Ties in Manchester. From left: Ashley Mallett, Tootal worker, Tootal promotions girl, Bill Lawry, Graham McKenzie and Paul Sheahan.

A famous SA cricketing group. From left: Eric Freeman, Les Favell, Ian Chappell, Victor Richardson, Ashley Mallett, Sir Donald Bradman, Barry Jarman, Clarrie Grimmett, Neil Hawke, Gef Noblet.
[Courtesy South Australian Tattersalls Club]

Bill Lawry introduces the author, Ashley Mallett, to the Queen, Lord's, June 1968. To Mallett's right is Les Joslin and to Joslin's right, John Inverarity.
[Ashley Mallett collection]

Ayr Cricket Club's professional cricketer-cum-groundsman Ashley Mallett on the morning of his Benefit Match at Cambusdoon, Scotland, 1967.
From Left: Adzil Holder (West Indies), Eddie Fuller (South Africa), author, Ian Johnstone (Ayr CC captain), 'General' John Grant (Victoria) and Peter Kelly (WA).
[Ashley Mallett collection]

Presentation of Whitbread Brewery dray to Ian Chappell's Australian team by Whitbread executive and Gloucester CCC president Frank Twistleton, 1972. From left: Paul Sheahan, Brian Taber, Twistleton, Mike Proctor, Sadiq, author, Bruce Francis and Chappell.

The return of SA representatives of World Series Cricket to the SA State team. From Left: Ian Chappell, David Hookes, Rodney Hogg, Howard Mutton (State coach), author, Peter Sleep and Rick Darling at Adelaide Oval, October, 1979. [Ashley Mallett collection]

Chapter 24

Jonny's band of courage

England's ebullient wicketkeeper-batsman Jonny Bairstow is probably the most courageous international player going around. It's not merely standing up to the pace and fire of bowlers such as Mitchell Starc or Josh Hazelwood in the heat of battle, nor keeping to an array of bowlers under a blazing Australian summer of Ashes cricket that makes Bairstow stand out. Jonny's greatest fight – a fight within – began when he was just a boy, yearning to one day play cricket for Yorkshire and/or football for Leeds United.

His story should be told right now and to all future generations of cricketers. Australians love an enthusiastic, combative cricketer, especially one who wears his heart on his sleeve. Jonny Bairstow's story of rising from the ashes of utter despair to becoming a wonderful wicketkeeper–batsman for Yorkshire and England is one of sheer determination and love amidst a childhood shattered by his father's suicide. David Bairstow died alone in the family home. He had hanged himself from the staircase. It was a cold, black January night in 1998 when Jonny, his mother Janet and sister Becky returned home from Jonny's football training at Leeds United to unimaginable shock and horror. David Bairstow was just 46, Jonny was eight years old. His dad, his hero, was gone. The family's grief was unimaginable. For years Jonny kept searching for an answer. Jonny's book, *A Clear Blue Sky* (Harper Collins), written in conjunction with top-flight writer Duncan Hamilton, is all of these things: eulogy, unofficial inquest, a record of uncompromising love and loyalty and the manner in which David's grieving family somehow rose above the sheer horror to get on with their lives. No one who knew David 'Bluey' Bairstow will forget him.

I met Bluey in 1980, during my last big match, the Centenary Test at Lord's. Bluey was England's 'keeper in that match, one of four Tests he was to play. A feisty, solid little bloke with a big heart he gave his all on the field and joined us for a beer and plenty of laughs off it. There's something endearing about Yorkshiremen. They play hard and they are never backward in telling you how it is. Never. Bluey was the embodiment of everything Yorkshire. Two Yorkies I know and admire – Geoff Boycott and (Sir) Michael Parkinson – are poles apart in just about everything except when it comes to Yorkshire itself, the place they call 'God's Own Country'. The Yorkies love their cricket and they love winning. They are brilliant scrappers and if you had to have a fellow soldier alongside you in trench warfare, you couldn't go past Bluey Bairstow, or indeed his son, Jonny.

Nine years after the Centenary Test at Lord's, my next sighting of Bluey was in South Africa, on the occasion of the republic celebrating 100 years of Test cricket. Quite a bizarre celebration really given 1989 was more than 18 years into South Africa's international sporting isolation and they had not turned out in an official Test match since 1970. Bluey and I were in the same Golden Oldies team led by Tony Greig. The team included the likes of Graham McKenzie, Dennis Amiss and Norman Gifford. The games were unimportant, but the great thing was I got to spend time with Bluey. We were there in March and Jonny was born on 26 September that same year.

A fun-loving lovely couple, Janet and Bluey Bairstow were like two peas in a pod, always sporting a smile, enjoying life. I got the feeling that Bluey was so Yorkshire he was indestructible. I was wrong. Time froze when I heard the shocking news of David's death. Must have been a year later that I picked up the newest edition of *Wisden*, in which Mathew Engel had written in tribute: 'Reports said he had been suffering from depression: his wife was ill, he had financial troubles, he faced a drink-driving charge and was in pain from his own injuries. The news stunned cricket, especially as Bairstow had always seemed the most indomitable and least introspective of men.'

How proud he would be of Jonny, whose 52-Test career (at the time of writing) has brought him 3293 runs, including five centuries (167 not out his best) at an average of 39.20, plus 129 catches and four stumpings. In 42 ODIs Jonny has a batting average of 48.36.

Jonny displayed his brilliant Yorkshire humour that day in the Perth Test when he brought up his Test century with a raising of the bat and a mischievous little head-butt of his helmet. I know Bluey would be over the moon with his son's cricket and the way he plays the game.

If someone you know needs help, contact LIFELINE on 13 11 54 or Lifeline.org.au or Beyond Blue on 1300 22 4636

Chapter 25

The 12th Man: the full story

Billy Birmingham is The 12th Man: the most famous 12th man of the cricket world. Conceived, written and performed by Billy, The 12th Man put out seven albums and three singles – and all went straight to number one on the charts. Billy sold more than two million recordings. He is the ultimate star on the sidelines: cricket's king of 12th men. He takes off Richie Benaud to a tee and looks like a slimmer version of Doc Emmett L. Brown, the eccentric character of the epic movie, *Back to the Future*. Perhaps he's that little bit zanier than the Doc, but Billy's proved to be just as smart, maybe smarter. Billy can't turn the clock back or forward, but as a performer he is ahead of his time.

The 12th Man takes the piss out of the Channel Nine cricket commentary team generally, concentrating on the former key man, Richie Benaud, cricket legend, commentary icon, but also taking the piss out of long-term stalwarts Ian Chappell, Bill Lawry, whose passion for pigeons is almost outmatched by his habit of overstating the ordinary (a forward defence sometimes has Bill on the edge of his seat with excitement), and the late Tony Greig, 'who keeps leaving the fucking keys stuck in the pitch'.

In his epic album, *The Final Dig?*, Billy explored the candidates for Richie Benaud's spot as commentary team captain, once the great man finally gave it away.

I was trying to do Tubby (Mark) Taylor for the first time, so I put down some stuff on tape and it worked okay, but then I hit on the idea of speeding up the tape, lots of words crammed into a short space and it sounded completely ridiculous, just the way I wanted it to sound.

I immediately thought of that splendid anti-nuclear demonstrator and lobbyist Dr Helen Caldicott, who talks with the speed of a pneumatic drill. The rate of her talking was such that I couldn't get a word down on paper during that interview for News Limited. The speed with which Tubby Taylor speaks in *The Final Dig?* gives the recording an added dimension of humour. Taking the piss out of almost every situation in life is Billy's way. And while he had taken the piss out of Richie Benaud for such a long time, it was 15 years before the two men met – and that was by chance – at Kennington Oval, London, in 1999. Billy was in England to promote his albums, parts of which had been adapted and re-recorded to 'suck up' to a potential new audience in the UK.

Billy was standing outside the Hallowed BBC commentary box waiting to speak to Jonathan Agnew, former England fast bowler and now BBC radio cricket commentator, when Billy heard the distinctive voice in the background, unmistakably Benaud.

> I turned around and saw this bloke, the unmistakable hair, the bottom lip. But he was somehow shorter than I imagined and he wore glasses. He wasn't wearing the cream, the bone, the white, the off-white, the ivory or the beige ... Richie was speaking on a mobile phone. And just as he was about to head back to the inner sanctum, I thought we should meet. It was about time. I decided to introduce myself. I jumped in front of him and blurted, 'Hey, Richie, some things you can't put off forever.' I stuck my hand out and said, 'How are you going?' Richie looked at me and said matter-of-factly, 'What a strange place to be meeting you. Ah, weren't we supposed to play golf together some time ago?' I replied in the affirmative and then said, 'Well, let's do it soon,' Richie replied, 'Well, from what I hear my game would have to improve out of sight before I took you on,' and with that he was off back to the combox.'

How did it all start? Well, let's start at the very beginning. Billy Birmingham was born at the Mater Hospital, Crow's Nest, on 5 July 1953 and his early years were spent living in Dee Why on Sydney's northern beaches. His mother Faye and father Colin were already proud parents of a girl, Prue, who was born 15 months before Billy. Colin Birmingham was in the rag trade, he sold cloth. Billy began his formal education at a Dee Why primary convent school. At the age of 10, Billy experienced a huge upheaval in his young life. He was sent to St Aloysius College at Milson's Point (near Luna Park and the Sydney Harbour Bridge). Billy found it both an adventure and rather traumatic to have to ride in a bus some 30 km every day from Dee Why to St Aloysius College, but eventually he adapted to his situation, if not entirely getting used to it. 'I was only ten years old. Here I was in third class dragged from the bosom of the nuns at Dee Why. It took me a while to adjust.'

But adjust he did. He was soon taking the piss out of the teachers at school. Billy used to answer teachers by imitating their voices. He was taking the piss without any of them really knowing. They seemed either so taken aback that they didn't retaliate or became confused, oblivious to the piss-taking yet knowing something was up.

The Birmingham home in Dee Why was always full of music. Billy loved music, always has loved music and he was brought up with Johnny O'Keeffe, the Rolling Stones, the Beatles and so on. The family would watch those old favourites on telly, such as the *Jackie Gleeson Show*, the *Red Skelton Show*, *Laugh-In* and other comedy shows. Billy found himself always impersonating voices. It began as long ago as Billy can remember. Impersonating and taking the piss out of individuals and situations came naturally to Billy Birmingham. Billy got his HSC (High School Certificate), but a tragedy was about to befall the Birmingham family.

Prue, Billy's sister, was in a car accident. She suffered severe injuries and brain damage, lying in a comatose state for a year. The enormous family tragedy weighed heavily on everyone and Billy found himself drifting apart from his parents. Prue Birmingham made a remarkable recovery and despite her irreversible disability she represented Australia as a multi-medal-winning disabled swimmer, with gold, silver and bronze in Japan and Holland. Meantime Billy had no idea what he wanted to do in work or in life.

Initially Billy undertook a hotel and catering management course at

Sydney Technical School. After three months he'd had enough. Billy's father suggested Billy seek work in an advertising firm. Billy went to school with John Doorley, and John's father Garth ran a small advertising agency. Billy was in. Had it been a big agency such as George Patersons Billy reckons he would have been wrapping parcels for two to three years, but because it was a small agency Billy got to do the whole damned business, from wrapping parcels to writing copy, getting to know the process of creating an advertisement in press or for the electronic media from start to finish: the idea, the copy, the creation of the image, be it a photograph or sketch, to completion.

However, Billy soon got restless. The work was okay, but the money was poor. He needed money to keep his car on the road, to help him live the life he wanted in relative comfort. So for three or four years, during the early great stress for the Birmingham family over Prue's terrible predicament, Billy entered the world of door-to-door selling.

He sold anything and everything from pots and pans to kitchen gadgets and adding machines. The jobs paid a retainer plus commission and Billy reckoned he could get through until the end-of-week sales conference, whereupon his sales figures were put under scrutiny. That day was not the best part of the week for him. He got the sack from many of the door-to-door sales jobs.

Some sort of stability came with selling movie screen advertising for Val Morgan. During those three to four years Billy drifted. It was, for him, a hugely confusing time. He was losing connection with his family as Prue, quite understandably, had been almost the total focus of his parents. But Billy hung in with the selling jobs, because he was out on the road and had no boss breathing down his neck. Then came 1975, an important year for Billy Birmingham. He was looking at the situations vacant columns in the *Sydney Morning Herald* when an advertisement for the ideal job jumped out, calling for someone with the unique combination of business acumen and a passion for music.

Billy decided that this was the job for him but reckoned that some 400 people would apply and only the person with a brilliantly different application would get a look in. He wrote an application letter which basically told the company that 'you guys are fucked if you don't employ Billy Birmingham', for he was the ideal bloke to be the NSW Promotions Manager for EMI Records. He duly got the job and found out that his instincts were right; in excess of 400 people had applied for the role. Billy knew this was an industry where he fitted perfectly. He would be promoting artists on the EMI label to radio stations and the media. He knew he would love the position.

On his first day he was invited to a party that night to celebrate the launch of Little River Band's first album.

Billy remembered:

> We were at some club in Oxford Street, Sydney. Glen Shorrock sidles up to me and says, 'Now, where have I met you?' And I said, 'Well, unless I sold you some kitchen gadgets or some cookware or a cash register, I don't think we have met.' Glen and I are still mates 30 years later and we still laugh over that first encounter.

Billy picked up the business swiftly and settled in for a good two-year stint. Then Radio 2GB, a struggling part of the Macquarie Network, decided to change its format overnight. They persuaded three Adelaide personalities at radio 5KA in Adelaide – Paul Thomson, Barry Bissell and Vince Lovegrove – to bring their entire format to Sydney. Radio 2GB would drop its racing format and croon-style music of Perry Como and others and become a rock station. Billy serviced the station so well they offered him a job as 2GB's promotions director. Things worked well for three months until senior management mysteriously decided to switch the format back to horse racing and Perry Como-style music. Messrs Thomson, Bissell, Lovegrove and Birmingham were offered the opportunity to stay on at 2GB under the new format. All four resigned on the spot.

The music business, however, was a passion for Billy and he soon met up with an old advertising mate, David 'Froggy' Froggatt, who had sold ads with him at Val Morgan. Froggy was a brilliant guitarist and had reached the stage where he wanted to branch out and get his band – Aleph – on the circuit. Billy, who now had spare time on his hands, was helping the band to secure a recording deal through his industry connections but soon found himself pretty much managing the band. Driving a Kombi van and dealing with venue managers and PA systems eventually started to give him the shits. On the same day that his car blew up in some obscure town in Victoria, Billy heard news that his father had passed away. He rushed back to Sydney to comfort his mum and sister. Fed up with life on the road, and feeling that he needed to be around his mum and sister at this time, Billy took a job as a greenkeeper at Northbridge Golf Club, on Sydney's leafy North Shore and replaced the dead Kombi van with a huge Pontiac Parisienne motor car, a beaten-up, souped up V-8-cylinder 'Yank Tank'.

After nine months of getting fit and keeping the golf club greens in great shape, Billy was having a beer after work when he ran in to John Doorley, the bloke whose father ran the small advertising agency. John offered Billy a job back at the agency, where he could be production manager and in quiet moments they could throw their joint creative energies into looking for new business, accounts that would be good fun and possibly bring in a big dollar. A car came with the offer (timely as the Pontiac's wheel dropped off as the car hit 60 km/h on the Pacific Highway) so Billy accepted.

He was back in the advertising business and stayed for two years until 1979. He also decided that EMI Records, his old employer, could do a lot worse than have him do their advertising through his small agency, and he eventually convinced them to give the boys the account. After a couple of years Billy realised there was not the time to do the sort of creative things he and John Doorley wanted to do, so he quit and started out on his own. *I went freelance and started Billy Birmingham and Associates. My first and only account was EMI Records, which I took with me when I left the agency.*

Billy was doing the whole thing himself. He grabbed an idea and ran with it, writing the copy, organising production. Already Billy had become something of a sensation among his mates. Sunday afternoons was barbecue time, and Billy entertained his friends by taking off various well-known characters. Richie Benaud, who arrived in everyone's lounge-room when World Series Cricket was thrust upon an unsuspecting cricket world, was the perfect target for Billy. He thought Benaud had such a strange-sounding, unique voice that he couldn't resist taking the piss out of it. At one barbecue, Billy was approached by a tall, burly, loud bloke, whom Billy hardly knew. Sandy Gutman wanted Billy to help him get into comedy and so invited him to his place so they could discuss how Billy might help. Sandy made Billy a cup of tea and Vegemite toast.

Billy and Sandy clicked immediately. Billy soon realised that Sandy's sense of humour was such that it even encroached upon his ability to make a decent cup of tea. Sandy's tea was dreadful. Perhaps his philosophy was akin to that of many a 12th man who has spilt the drinks on purpose in the hope of never again being lumbered with the job. Billy went on a fact-finding-cum-holiday mission to the US. He checked out the comedy scene on the strip and when he returned to Australia he discovered Sandy had auditioned for the Sydney Comedy Store and was rattling off one-liners, many of which were Billy Birmingham specials ...

> *How much can a koala bear?*
> *I'll go if dingoes ...*
> *Nullabors me shitless ...*
> *Will wallaby there?*
> *Yeah, and vegemite come to ...*

Gutman was six foot four inches tall, and big. He was an affronting and abrasive comedian, so his stage name needed to reflect both his bulk and his personality. Billy hit upon the handle, Austen Tayshus. If the one-liners were working for his comedian, Billy reckoned it might work better if he could get lots of the one-liners into a make-sense story, the lots of little stories fitting a pattern. He decided to write a script, called *Australiana*, for Austen Tayshus.

> I grabbed a sheet of paper and an HB pencil and went out to the backyard, sat down and wrote *Australiana*. The pen started flowing straight away and I found I had pretty much written the whole thing in 45 minutes.

The result was a series of puns, some fair, some foul, of a monologue so brilliant that it became a record and spent 13 weeks at number one in Australia, beaten in almost 50 years of Australian chart history by only two other acts, The Beatles and Abba, who held the number one spot for 15 weeks. Austen Tayshus's *Australiana* sold more than 300,000 copies, the biggest domestic-selling Australian single of all time.

At this stage of his career, Billy was in the background. He wrote the 'How do you feel?' radio campaign for Tooheys, winning a truckload of awards, and he was a commercial producer and commercial creative consultant. The time was nigh for Billy Birmingham to star.

> The year was 1984. I was thinking about how I could capitalise on the success of Australiana. What could I do? I thought of Richie Benaud and the boys. Then I hit upon the idea of trying to do something with my lounge-room impersonations of them, maybe taking the piss out of the Channel Nine cricket coverage. I put down the stuff on a dictaphone. And right on cue a few mates turned up at the end of the day and said, 'What have you been doing?' I pressed the play button on the dictaphone and said 'Listen to this?' Someone said, 'Fuck, you've got to do something with this.'

The tape, which soon had the title *It's Just Not Cricket*, ran for seven minutes. Billy knew he was on to something special, he had received the unanimous thumbs up from his mates, ever the strongest of critics.

> I immediately shot down to EMI Records. I recall going in to the boss's office and I turned on the cassette. It was just the raw thing, no music, no special effects, just me taking the piss out of Richie and the Pakistanis. The EMI boss's door was open and as we listened and he laughed, others heard the commotion. One by one they came in until the room was full, everyone was laughing. The EMI boss said, 'Let's go with this.'

Billy was amazed that the various radio stations played his record *It's Just Not Cricket*. Usually and traditionally they stuck to a musical format. Billy considers himself to be a satirist, not an impressionist nor an impersonator.

> I like to get the voice right, but it's hard to get it perfect – so long as the characterisation is accurate enough not to distract from the script. What the bloke says is important. How he says it is also important and that the voice is near as possible to the real thing, but what he says, that's the really important factor for me.

How did Billy hit upon the title, *The 12th Man*?

> I was watching Stuart McGill, 12th man in Durban. There he was sitting back, head to one side, a book cradled in the crook of his arm. He was filling in time

while the other eleven guys were slogging it out in the middle. The 12th Man has lots of time on his hands. He can just sit there and take the piss: that's me!

Billy and his mate, David 'Froggy' Froggatt produced the records at Froggy's home studio in Bowral, Don Bradman's spiritual home town in the Southern Highlands of NSW. Billy said the recording process 'took several weeks of fear and loathing and eating pizzas and staying up ungodly hours, putting down hundreds of voices and sound effects'.

The 12th Man series took Australia by storm. It was different, outrageous and, above all, took the piss out of an icon in a fun way. The recipe was right. It fitted the mood of the Australian public. Those soaring sales figures revealed the extent of its popularity. In February 1992, the musical single 'Marvellous' by The 12th Man, featuring MCG Hammer (as well as premier league rock heroes Jimmy Barnes, Glen Shorrock and Diesel) was number-one platinum single. In December of the same year, a third album, *Still The 12th Man*, became the fastest-selling Australian artist recording EMI had ever handled, selling more than 200,000 units in a matter of weeks. The fourth album, released in December 1994, *Wired World of Sports II*, won the ARIA for the highest selling album and best comedy album.

***

Some familiarity with the pronunciation of the names of the Subcontinent would help the reader get an immediate handle on the way Billy fashions his Pakistani, Sri Lankan and Indian names, so constructed to form a clever line. The common Pakistani surname KHAN, is pronounced 'Carn'. There is also AHMED IMINAGAYBAR from Pakistan, which translates to 'I met him in a gay bar'. Work the others out yourself. Still from Pakistan: ARBROKE MIANDAD, JIWADA WAQAR and WASI AKRIM. From Sri Lanka there is the opening pair AFIL LARKACHUNDA and AHMAD NEEDAPUTU and the gob-smacking AQUIB MATEEF INAJARBESIDEDABED.

The opening batting pair for India in the 1980s were CUTEEZ ARMINARF and SUNIL HAVASKAR. Other prominent Indians included ADONNA KHAN SINGH and ARIL MADAFARKAR. The piss-taking cricketing names of the Subcontinent made people laugh the world over. They are still making people laugh. Anyone who is serious about saying 'two' in the funniest way has got to become a cult figure. Billy Birmingham simply struck the right chord; the nation's fun pulse. He got it right first time and he continues to get it right. Funny thing is that Richie Benaud himself was quite adept at taking the piss. And he wasn't afraid to drop the odd 'F' word off camera. I read that Richie's wife Daphne said Billy had got Richie down to a tee.

Chapter 26

Charlie Puckett: Iron Man

Charlie Puckett was a legend of Western Australian cricket and Australian baseball. In baseball he played Claxton Shield for WA and SA and was named an all-Australian in 1948 and 1952. Puckett was a stockily built man, just under six feet in height, sporting a barrel chest and powerful forearms. He had a magnificent throwing arm and was both a catcher and pitcher in baseball. In Puckett's time, baseball was played in the winter months and many cricketers played baseball in the off-season to keep fit for cricket. As a medium-paced bowler he played 37 first-class matches for WA and was said to have been on the cusp of being selected in Don Bradman's 1948 Australian team's tour of England, the team that became universally known as The Invincibles.

In the summer of 1947–48 Puckett bowled unchanged for two-and-half hours to bring victory to WA over Queensland at the Gabba. Late in the day he turned the match on its head, taking the last five Queensland wickets for nine runs in six explosive overs. WA bowled out Queensland on the final day for 130 (Puckett 6/48) and that victory brought the state its first Sheffield Shield.

Puckett was a strong, lion-hearted sportsman who kept on keeping on through thick and thin. He was indefatigable as a bowler and when the ball lost its shine and hardness, he would revert to bowling slow-medium off cutters and quickish off breaks. As he promised his WA captain Keith Carmody at the Gabba that defining day in February 1948, he was always prepared to bowl 'until my arm drops off'. So it was not only his habit of stopping the ball with his shins that earned Puckett the nickname, The Iron Man.

Charlie's dad was a one-time curator at Kennington Oval, Surrey County Cricket Club's famous home ground. Charlie was born in Beddington Corner, Surrey, England, in 1911, and when he was a boy the family sailed to Australia and settled in Adelaide. His baseball prowess blossomed and in 1938 he was lured to Perth to play baseball for WA. Puckett had already made his name as a catcher for South Australia and Victoria. Two of his brothers also developed into star baseballers and his son, Max, who died in 1991, was a five-times all-Australian. Max also played one Sheffield Shield match for South Australia (versus Western Australia in the summer of 1964–65).

To Charlie, cricket was little more than a summer's diversion away from his main sport, but in 1939–40 he was selected in a match for WA against SA and he got a few wickets, one of whom was Don Bradman. Puckett was the first bowler to take 100 wickets for WA in Sheffield Shield cricket. In the 1947–48 summer he took 5/56 and 6/78 against India in Perth and his 24 wickets at 24.79 was instrumental in WA's victory in its debut Sheffield Shield summer. Playing just four matches in 1949–50 Puckett took 32 wickets at 18.87 and was picked in Bill Brown's Australian team to tour New Zealand (considered a second XI because Australia at the time did not recognise NZ as a genuine Test match country).

On the morning of 14 June 2018 I rang Alan Davidson, the great all-rounder who toured New Zealand with Brown's Australian XI. He said of Puckett: 'Charlie was a good cricketer and a champion bloke. Norm O'Neill had a wonderful throwing arm but Charlie, he had the greatest throwing arm, so good it left Normie for dead.'

In 1951–52 Puckett got 5/45 against a good West Indies team and a season later he grabbed 5/119 against a powerful South African team in Perth. It is a pity that Puckett didn't play Test cricket. He had the likes of Ray Lindwall, Bill Johnston and Keith Miller – all proven champion fast bowlers – standing in his way. However, Charlie Puckett won many plaudits and the respect of all those cricketers who played with and against him. He was also honoured with a place in Australian Baseball's Hall of Fame.

In 1958 Charlie coached the Nedlands Baseball Club's Under-16 team. My brother Nick, two years my elder, and yours truly played in that side. I was going on 13 and rarely got a full game.

From the outset I found catching the ball often resulted in a bruised left thumb. Charlie soon put that right and he stuck me at right field; not too many fly balls came my way that first season. Nick was one of the team pitchers, along with the star thrower of the day, Baden Pratt, a brother of all-Australian Neville. Funny how things turn out. Baden became a journalist with the *Daily News* in Perth, Nick played as a pitcher for both WA and Victoria, and I gave up baseball because it became a summer sport and I turned to cricket. But in that winter of 1958, Charlie Puckett taught us a few tricks and one terrific reality check. If you skied a ball and the opposing catcher was standing under it Charlie would tell us to fake losing our balance or make out we'd suddenly developed a state of disorientation, which caused us to fall all over the catcher thus making him drop the ball. When we started to beat all comers and were getting cocky, Charlie organised an opposing team to play a bunch of 17 and 18 year olds. He reckoned we needed – and he was right – to lose a game if we were going to move on to winning the flag. We lost the game, but won the premiership.

At the age of 48, Charlie was invited to turn out for the Fremantle Braves under lights at the WACA. All of us, the blokes who played for Nedlands in winter and the Fremantle Braves in summer, had heard of Charlie Puckett's legendary status in the game, his strong and powerful arm. Well, we discovered firsthand how good he was then and how brilliant he must have been in his prime. Charlie was on his haunches behind the home plate awaiting the next pitch. A fellow on first base was looking cocky and eager to steal second base. The runner was a long way off first, but the pitcher didn't try and peg him with a throw to first; he fired the ball at Puckett. The runner must have been halfway to his destination when Charlie caught the ball. Without getting off his haunches Charlie fired a rocket-like throw to second and the runner was tagged, sliding into the second baseman's glove. Gone for all money. There was a collective sigh among the crowd.

In any other era, the Iron Man could have played Test cricket or Major League Baseball in the US. The war years robbed him, as they robbed many a great sportsmen, of their best years. Instead of being an unarmed combat instructor for the Australian Army ... what might have been? When he got the opportunity Charlie Puckett was pretty special. Charlie died in South Australia in 2002 aged 90, truly an Australian sporting legend.

Chapter 27

Bodyline Adelaide

On Saturday 14 January 1933, all hell broke loose at Adelaide Oval. The man who executed England captain Douglas Jardine's Bodyline attack (designed to quell the brilliance of Don Bradman) was fast bowler Harold Larwood. On this black Saturday Larwood struck Australian captain Bill Woodfull a fearful blow to the heart, and the crowd became an angry mob after wicketkeeper Bill Oldfield was knocked out by a hit to the temple. Only swift and expert horsemanship by dozens of mounted police prevented the crowd from storming the ground and attacking the villains of the piece – Jardine and Larwood.

It was the height of The Depression. Thousand were out of work. On 9 January 1931 hundreds of unemployed men fought a pitched battle with police in the Adelaide CBD over a protest against cuts in dole rations. With Jardine's men in town, the police expected trouble. On the first day of the Test mounted troopers were in position in the Adelaide Oval No 2 Ground. England scored 341, but the day passed quietly. So too the early part of day two until Don Bradman joined Woodfull.

Just after stumps England team managers Pelham 'Plum' Warner and Richard Palairet went to the Australian dressing room to offer Woodfull an apology. Woodfull was unusually curt and said that he did not wish to see them: 'There are two teams out there. One is trying to play cricket and the other is not. The game is too good to be spoilt. It is time some people got out of it. Good afternoon!'

Woodfull's comment was leaked by someone in the dressing room. Bradman always blamed Jack Fingleton. There were only two others present in the room at the time Woodfull made the comment, 12th man Leo O'Brien and a room attendant everyone thought to be stone deaf.

Woodfull's words attacked the very foundations of cricket, established by the forefathers of a visibly hurt Pelham Warner and smarting Marylebone Cricket Club official crying into their stiff gins back at Lord's. Lord's was further incensed by a cable from the Australian Cricket Board for International Control:

BODYLINE BOWLING HAS ASSUMED SUCH PROPORTIONS AS TO MENACE THE BEST INTERESTS OF THE GAME, MAKING PROTECTION OF THE BODY BY THE BATSMAN THE MAIN CONSIDERATION. THIS IS CAUSING INTENSELY BITTER FEELINGS BETWEEN THE PLAYERS AS WELL AS INJURY. IN OUR OPINION IT IS UNSPORTSMANLIKE. UNLESS STOPPED AT ONCE IT IS LIKELY TO UPSET FRIENDLY RELATIONS BETWEEN BRITAIN AND AUSTRALIA.

It seemed heads would roll. Clarrie Grimmett, who came to SA after years seeking recognition of his art, found Adelaide to be the haven for unwanted bowlers and the staging post for England. He took a modest 3/168 off 63 overs for the match, but no one expected the great leg-spinner to be unceremoniously dumped for the rest of the series.

Clarrie Grimmett never publicly came under suspicion, despite his reputation as an opportunist with the media. He took movie and still film during his three tours of England, especially on the 1930 and 1934 tours, and made a lot of money in 1930 selling his film to the highest bidder. The Board may have suspected Grimmett spilt the beans. The Adelaide Bodyline Test was Grimmett's last big game on Australian soil. He was picked for the 1934 tour of England and took 25 wickets in the five Tests; then he toured South Africa with Vic Richardson's Australian team, taking a record 44 wickets at an average of 14 – and inexplicably never played Test cricket again.

The Bodyline strategy began just before the 1932–33 England team sailed to Australia in quest of the Ashes. At a secret meeting in a London hotel Jardine outlined his plan to his key fast bowler, Harold Larwood:

Jardine asked me if I could bowl on the leg stump making the ball come up into the body all the time, so that Bradman had to play his shots to leg. 'Yes, I think that can be done,' I said ... I had no doubt of its purpose: we thought Don was frightened of sharp rising balls, and we reasoned that if he got a lot of them he would be ... intimidated and eventually, having to direct his shots to leg all the time, would give a catch to one of the [leg-side] fieldsmen.

Larwood, who played cricket as a profession, simply agreed. He followed orders.

Others opposed Jardine; men such as Gubby Allen, vice captain Bob Wyatt, Wally Hammond and Les Ames, but for the two fast men, Larwood and Bill Voce, men who found their way out of the drudgery of the coal mine to play Test cricket, relished the Bodyline plan and used it to telling effect. With no restriction on how many men were stationed behind square leg, Larwood and Voce were relentless in their use of short-pitched bowling, aiming every ball at the chest and head.

Well-travelled Robert Koehne of Carey Gully has found a different spin on Bodyline through his research into Indian culture while working for University SA encouraging students in India to study in SA. 'I found that one of the England players vehemently opposed to Jardine's Bodyline tactics, Ifthikar Ali Khan, the Nawab of Pataudi, was axed from the team because of his stand.' Batting at number four, the Nawab of Pataudi hit a brilliant 102 on debut in the first Test at Sydney in December 1932.

Losing the first Test, Australia fought back to win the second match in Melbourne, but Pataudi's 'relationship with the haughty, supercilious and provocative Jardine had deteriorated' to the point of no return. When Pataudi refused to take his place in the Bodyline leg-trap, Jardine sneered, 'Ah, I see his Highness is a conscientious objector.' Jardine may have been a little confused by Pataudi's status on one hand and lifestyle as ruler of one of the 553 princely states. Many princes had accumulated huge fortunes over hundreds of years. With Indian Independence in 1947 successive socialist governments stripped the princes of their privileges.

Robert Koehne observed: 'Not being prepared for life in the real world, many squandered fortunes. Many of their palaces are now heritage-style hotels, giving tourists a glimpse of the old, sybaritic lifestyles.'

Years after Bodyline, in 1946, Pataudi captained India on a tour of England. He remains the only cricketer to represent both England and India on the Test stage.

In 1969 I toured India with Bill Lawry's Australian side and the son of the man who defied Jardine, Mansur Ali Khan, the latest Nawab of Pataudi. He was a good captain and despite the loss of his right eye, Pataudi was a fine batsman and probably an even better captain.

Ian Chappell once asked Tiger Pataudi: 'As a prince what do you do?'

He smiled: 'I'm a prince. I don't do anything.'

Bodyline is a distant memory, but some immortal lines remain. When Jardine was swatting flies at an Ashes Test on the SCG in that series, famous barracker Yabba yelled: 'Leave our flies alone Jardine ... they're the only friends you've got here.'

And one for the ages: 'Jardine, I wish you were a statue and I was a pigeon.'

Chapter 28

Belief

The day was stiflingly hot and children from myriad schools stood about on a sun-drenched Sydney Cricket Ground awaiting the arrival of the Queen and the Duke of Edinburgh. Eventually the couple swept past our line in a black limousine. We had just enough time to see that out of the window appeared a right Royal white-gloved hand. Her Majesty gave a few gentle swishes of her hand and then she was gone.

It was February 1954 and I was then an eight-year-old student attending Chatswood Public School. The children were glad of a few hours away from school, albeit it was hot and we were thirsty, hungry and pretty much peeved that the Royals did but appear and then they disappeared. We were left standing waiting to be shunted back in line for the return bus trip to school. I felt somewhat cheated that one minute the Queen was there and then she was gone. As I write Queen Elizabeth is enjoying the 67th year of her reign. At least I got the chance to stand in the middle of the famous SCG. Over dinner that night I spoke about the experience: the SCG and Royalty. Don't know what was better, the cricket ground where so many wonderful players had performed – Trumper, Bradman, O'Reilly, Lindwall, Miller, Grimmett – or the Queen, about whom my mum devoured every word by a variety of Royal watchers covering the tour for the *Women's Weekly*.

'Now sit down, Ash, and eat your dinner,' Mum said. 'You can tell us all about it in a while ... don't talk with your mouth full.' She added with a smile: 'Now mind your table manners. You'll have to do just that when you sit down for dinner with the Queen at Buckingham Palace.'

From the age of six I wanted to become a Test cricketer. I was lucky enough to have an older brother, Nick, and he loved sport; cricket and rugby union, not necessarily in that order. He loved batting in the backyard and I always found myself bowling.

It was a good time after a rather rough initiation to crossing the road. We lived on busy Miller Street in Cammeray and it might well have been my first day at school, for I was just five years old. There we were standing on the footpath in front of our Sydney home when Nick suddenly declared: 'Beat you across the road.' Those backyard 'Tests' always brought me to the challenge, especially to mix it with the bigger kid. Nick beat me across the road by some six months for I was run over by a vehicle I later discovered to be an Oldsmobile. Rain was tumbling down and I recall seeing a number of colourful oil slicks on the wet road. One of them probably attributed to my slipping and sliding toward the middle of the road, one leg tucked in the other extended, and the big black car ran over my left thigh. Six months in the Royal North Shore Hospital was followed by nine months in a calliper and many trips to the physiotherapist. Mum was always there for me.

The six months in hospital taught me patience. I had no choice. But lying there with little to do in a ward full of youngsters with varying ailments also brought its rewards. Some of the kids got soft toys, best of all a tennis ball, when parents called to see them. When the nurses weren't about after we'd had lunch or tea and before 'lights out' it was on for young and old. Well, pretty young. The eldest was probably the ripe old age of eight. Soft toys and balls of all description were hurled about. We devised little games and competitions among us. Amazing how inventive youngsters, even ones of tender age, can be when left to their own devices. Six months is a fair time span for a boy of five and I rarely had visits from my parents less than a week apart. I found I had to make my own fun.

Hospital for me could have come much sooner. When I was four we lived in a lovely split-level home in Chatswood on Sydney's North Shore. Upstairs was the living quarters, bedrooms, bathrooms, lounge room and kitchen. Downstairs was a huge play area, spacious laundry and toilet. One day I was playing alone when I noticed the sweep of a dark shadow out of the corner of my eye. It was a big black cat, bigger by far than the usual domestic cat of my experience. Suddenly the cat sprang from the floor of the laundry to the top of the washing machine. It was making a low, growling sound. We had outside stairs and from the kitchen window mum could see where I was on the patio leading to the laundry. I called to her for milk, the big cat needed a drink. Mum came down the stairs with a bowl of sour milk, perfect for a thirsty cat.

But when mum saw the cat moving towards her four-year-old son sitting beside the bowl of milk she called to my father: 'Ray, come here. I don't look the look of this.' From the kitchen window they could see me cradling the head of the cat as it greedily lapped up the milk. The cat had a large head for a domestic animal and huge, round yellow eyes.

'Clare,' he said, 'just heard on the wireless. A panther has escaped from Wirth's Circus ... in Chatswood.' Dad rang the police. The panther had its fill and dashed off into the scrub and within an hour a bloke in jodhpurs, army-issue khaki shirt, holding a whip in one hand, in the other a net, stood before us.

'I see you've got that big cat. Was it any danger to the young'un?' asked Dad.

'Well the panther is only three months old, but it is powerful enough to take you, mate,' the circus trainer snapped.

Perhaps the panther sensed I wouldn't harm it and that I displayed no sign of fear. I guess that's it. When you are young you feel bullet proof. We learn about fear later on. In hospital I wasn't afraid, just lonely for the company of my family. You tend to develop your imagination and live vicariously. Those cricketers I'd heard about, Keith Miller and Richie Benaud, come to mind for there I was either suddenly transformed into a Miller or a Benaud doing great things before a bumper crowd on the SCG. Funny how I picked those blokes. Maybe they were the most charismatic and I was one very shy little boy.

A few months after standing on the SCG to see the Royal couple my grandfather took me to the SCG to watch my first game of big cricket. We got the train in to the city and the bus to the ground and were there in plenty of time. There was tremendous excitement in the air for Neil Harvey was at the wicket and Australia needed less than 200 runs to win the Test. Pop, my granddad, loved his cricket. Victor Trumper, the great batsman before Don Bradman, was his favourite and he must have figured that this very day was the best day to introduce me to the big cricket. An Australian win was very much on the cards.

We settled on seats in front of the MA Noble stand; pretty much behind the wicket or slightly to the right, round the angle of fine third man. In came Frank Tyson, the man they called 'Typhoon', to bowl to Harvey and the left-hander hooked him to the fine-leg boundary. The crowed roared; we roared.

'Four runs less to get,' Pop enthused. A single next ball brought Graeme Hole to the crease.

'He's got a high back lift, this cove,' Pop said in a concerned tone, 'No yorkers please, Mr Tyson.'

Hole's bat had barely started its downswing when the searing Tyson yorker took out his middle stump, which cartwheeled back 20 yards to keeper Godfrey Evans.

Hole bowled Tyson 0.

With another right-hander on strike, there standing right in front of us was the young Colin Cowdrey, a ruddy-faced, classy 23-year-old batsman from Kent. He was so close to the fence I could have reached out to touch his sweater, but I dared not. In those days the field was sacrosanct and the players were veritable Gods of Olympus. Australia battled on against the pace of Tyson, who was bowling at breakneck speed. Only Harvey stood up to him with any sort of authority. Benaud, one of my heroes, came, hit a few fours before attempting an audacious slog off the Yorkshireman, off-spinner Bob Appleyard. The ball went a long way up and he left the wicket scoring only 12. Alan Davidson hardly bothered the scoreboard, nicking Tyson behind for Evans to complete an easy catch. Eventually the Australians were all out, 38 runs short. England had won. But two things came out of that extraordinary experience for me.

I got to see one of the great Test match innings by Neil Harvey and I saw a Test cricketer within arm's reach. And fate took a hand, for Cowdrey became my first Test wicket, at Kennington Oval in August 1968, some 14 years later.

THWACK!

In 1955 the Mallett family packed up in Sydney and sailed to Perth in the P&O liner *Stratheden*, an ex-troop carrier during WWII. To Nick and I it was akin to being transported to the moon. The place seemed so far away, isolating, and what's more, you couldn't even get a Paddle Pop. But Nick and I settled in quickly. We were known as the latest 'Eastern Staters'. Western Australians were fiercely patriotic. Australian Rules Football was out for me because the players were 'off side'. At North Inglewood Primary School there was no rugby union team, but there was a soccer team and in the winter months I played soccer. The game was better to play than to watch, for goals were few and far between.

I can't remember much about the games, but I do recall our captain, Louis Devatimo. He was from an Italian migrant family and he always took the kick off to start the game. Louis booted the ball as far as he could. I swear he was trying to kick a goal from the centre first up. Mount Lawley High School didn't have a soccer team, but they did have a baseball team and I played that game in winter, probably following my brother Nick, who attended the school a couple of years before me and excelled in hockey and baseball.

Sport was everything to me at school. We played backyard Test matches at a friend's place because it had a spacious back garden. Matches were fierce affairs, albeit we bowled with a bald tennis ball and used a weather-beaten bat, complete with perished rubber-handle grip and enough broken edges to send Geoff Boycott away in tears. I recall Gavin McCoy, next-door neighbour, was there, as well as Evan Jones, the kid who sat next to me in class and was my closest rival in the 100-yard sprint championship at North Inglewood Primary and, of course, Don Moran. In backyard matches the kids wore a singlet or T-shirt, shorts and played barefooted. Moran turned up in creams, sprigged boots, proper pads, gloves and a brand-spanking new Norm O'Neill autographed Slazenger cricket bat. You can imagine what happened when Moran took guard. All the fieldsmen were hoping that a ball would hit Moran on the body – anywhere on the body and a raucous appeal would follow and five or six index fingers shoot skyward. Don Moran never changed his way. It was always the full cricket kit, never T-shirt and shorts. He always came dressed the part and after one or two balls he departed – hit anywhere on the body – LBW. We progressed with our cricket, joined clubs and David Cowlishaw even contemplated writing a cricket book with the working title, *Fourths from the Fence*.

I didn't like the formality of schoolwork and couldn't see the logic of learning algebra or physics. Neither subject interested me and I could not envisage how either would help me in whatever work I undertook when I left school. My dear old dad told me to 'aim for the stars ... and you might hit the treetops'.

In 1960, when I was about to enter the workforce, my Mount Lawley High School form teacher, Don Melrose, asked me what I was going to do. 'Now, you are just 15 and about to start work in a bank. Is that your life ambition?' he asked with a curious pursing of the lips.

'Well, Don. I am going to play Test cricket and I aim to become a good writer.'

'Ah,' his eyes narrowed and those pursed lips instantly became thin, brown lines. 'There is no money in cricket and writing is out because you are hopeless at English.' Mr Melrose was right on both counts: at that time, long before Kerry Packer rescued Test players by bringing television to the game, there was no money in cricket. And my English wasn't exactly tickety-boo. I couldn't fathom either the depth or the value of grammar in all its various pedantic forms.

Lunchtime at the bank was an eye opener. In summer the round table discussion embraced three main topics: sex, cricket and how to rob the bank. Winter was slightly different: sex, football and how to rob the bank. The bank taught me two things; it was a job I knew I didn't want to pursue, and it offered me an opportunity to regularly contribute to the bank's suggestion box. I wrote regularly. None of my suggestions, I might add, were ever taken up by the bank, but the exercise got me writing. Eventually I hit upon the idea that if one could articulate in speech then he, or she, should be able to write clearly and succinctly. Mark Nicholas is a fine example of someone who speaks eloquently and writes fluently.

Back in the mid 1960s I was bowling badly. Well, I wasn't too bad, just couldn't get many batsmen out. My dad said I was 'flighting the ball'. He was dead right, but it may have had something to do with a growth spurt I had in my early teens, growing 11 inches in 11 months. Once a little bloke tossing the ball, I was now a tall bloke and anything I tossed up was overpitched. At the age of 15, my spin bowling mate Terry Jenner and I were training at the WACA Ground in Perth. It happened to be the final day of the Australia–West Indies first Test of the 1960–61 series at the Gabba. In fact as TJ and I strolled away from the nets heading towards the dressing shed we noticed the players in the just completed Governor's Eleven versus an Invitation Eleven walking from the field. What we didn't notice was the hum of WA Governor Sir Charles Gardiner's gleaming black Rolls Royce moving slowly beside us. The car stopped, a door opened and Sir Charles sang out: 'Hop in, lads ... let's listen to the final stages of the match. Surely Australia must win!' Well, Australia didn't win, but we also didn't lose. It was, of course, the first tied Test in history. And there were two emerging spinners – Terry Jenner and Ashley Mallett – sitting in the luxurious comfort of Sir Charles's car listening to history unfold.

By the time I got into the Mount Lawley Cricket Club's A grade side I was in the team as an opening batsman, a good gully fieldsman and an off-spinner, who bowled tightly, albeit without too much flight. I rarely got wickets. In my three seasons in A grade with Mount Lawley I think 4/58 was my best haul. For a long time I thought I was a good bowler out of luck, then I came to the conclusion that no one can halve that much bad luck. I needed help.

At the age of 20 I thought time was starting to run out for me if I was to fulfil my ambition and became a Test cricketer. One day I found myself re-visiting an old cricket book, *A Century of Cricketers* by A.G. 'Johnny' Moyes (Angus & Robertson, Sydney, 1950). I read once more of the great cricketers – Victor Trumper, Don Bradman, Bill O'Reilly and then I honed in on Grimmett. His story of going from his native Wellington (NZ), to Sydney then Melbourne and finally finding fame in Adelaide, 'the haven for unwanted bowlers and the staging post for England', enthralled and inspired me. Maybe there was a chance to get a whole lot better a whole lot quicker. Anyone who could take 127 bags of five wickets or more in 248 first-class matches must have been some bowler. I needed to learn from this man – quickly. So I wrote to him. He wrote back in a lovely cursive hand wishing me well, but saying I should think about the following winter. 'The rains have come. It's cold, the grass is wet and I might bog the roller. Come next year, round early April.'

I got a few 70s for Mount Lawley, but continued to be a good bowler out of luck, even found myself WA 12th man for two games in the summer of 1966–67, at the end of which I again wrote to Mr Grimmett. It was arranged he would see me over a couple of days in the early April of 1967. Despite setbacks in form and lack of wickets I still had the belief that I would make good. I also wanted to repay Mum's unerring belief in me.

I believed that through Mr Grimmett's tuition I would find a way of becoming a Test match bowler. As the train pulled out of Perth Railway Station my real cricket journey had only just begun.

Chapter 29

Bingo!

Catching the train from Adelaide to Perth in 1967 was some sort of journey. First there was the trip from Perth to Kalgoorlie on a train, which would not have been out of place on the US railroads. The end carriage was an open affair, complete with iron guardrails and water bags hanging in the breeze. We disembarked at Kalgoorlie and boarded the Indian Pacific (on a different-sized gauge rail line) for the long trek (some 800 miles of spinifex, dust clouds and huge mobs of kangaroos on the horizon) across the Nullabor Plain. There was a third change of trains (and another gauge difference) for the trip from Port Augusta to Adelaide. My Mount Lawley spin twin, Terry Jenner, got off at Port Augusta. He had already decided to leave WA and would play for the Prospect Club in Adelaide. Meantime he was visiting a girl in Port Augusta and I was hell-bent upon learning about unlocking the mystery to this spin bowling business.

The trip took more than two days. Adelaide was not unfamiliar to me. How well I remember this City of Churches and the home of Don Bradman. Churches and Don Bradman. I had been there in 1958 as a member of the WA State Schoolboys' Cricket Team. During the trip I discovered a thorough dislike of lamb's fry, had my water pistol confiscated and soon got homesick. Mum always asked how many wickets I had taken, be it at training or in a match, and never enquired as to how many runs were scored from my bowling, so she was not surprised when she read of my taking 9/20 in the first innings of the match against NSW. Unsurprisingly she asked, 'Nine wickets, eh? Congratulations, Ash. How'd the other one get away?' Our opening bowler dismissed one of their batsmen before I was brought on so I was denied the chance to take all ten.

Once playing for Mount Lawley Under-16s at Shearn Park in Perth I took 8/9 and it should have been 9/5 but Baden Pratt at first slip not only did he drop the sitter of a catch, but the ball, having ricocheted off his chest, went to the boundary. It was all due to Baden having clapped his eyes on the pretty blonde walking down the street parallel to the play.

In no time at all I had caught a bus to the home of Clarrie Grimmett, the famous leg-spinner between the wars, first bowler in Test history to take 200 wickets. I knocked on the front door of his solid brick house in the leafy suburb of Firle, some 10 km from the CBD.

Mrs Grimmett (Lizzy) opened the door and immediately scolded her visitor: 'Get off the porch, I've just washed it!' She settled down when I hopped off her pristine porch and explained my presence.

'Mr Grimmett is out back,' she smiled, 'probably still high up in a peppercorn tree.'

As I walked round the back of the house I heard the familiar sound of someone sawing wood and as I wandered under the shade of the tree down jumped a 76-year-old leprechaun clutching a hand saw. Clarrie smiled warmly as we shook hands then turned to grab hold of the nearby Jack Hobbs' autographed cricket bat, which was leaning upright against the trunk of the tree. Brandishing it he said, 'Righto, let's have a look at your batting?'

I stumbled over my mild protest that I wasn't a batsman but a bowler who wanted to become much better at the art, but Clarrie would have none of it. The sawing was about Clarrie clearing branches on the peppercorn tree so the cricket ball hanging in one of Lizzy's stockings would not be impeded when the ball was struck with the Jack Hobbs' bat – *Thwack!*

He handed me the bat and said: 'Now, young man, pay attention. I taught a young man to back-cut on board ship on our way to England in 1930 and Don Bradman was a fast learner!'

I shaped up and Clarrie swung the ball towards me. I met the ball with the full face of the Jack Hobbs' bat. 'Righto, son. That's enough of your batting. Let's see if you can bowl.'

He led the way to a grassed enclosure, spacious enough for three or four turf pitches. The 76-year-old spin bowling legend took hold of the bat. He had no protection: no pads, abdominal protector, no gloves and was wearing horn-rimmed glasses. Facing up he said with a smile, 'Righto, bowl up.'

My first ball was right on song. It dipped a little and Clarrie came forward confidently and met it with the full face of his Jack Hobbs' bat. He called me down the pitch, 'Son, give up bowling and become a batsman! I could play you blindfolded.'

Wow, I was so deflated, but how could he judge so harshly after just one ball. I reached into my pocket. 'Blindfolded, eh? Well, Mr Grimmett, I have a handkerchief here.'

He took the handkerchief and placed it over his horn-rimmed glasses and settled down to receive another ball. Again I was super accurate. Clarrie met the ball with the full face of his Jack Hobbs bat – and when he stopped laughing proceeded to give me the best lesson on spin bowling I had ever experienced.

'Now Ashley,' Clarrie began, 'If you happened to be standing on a bridge overlooking a highway, would you be able to judge the speed of oncoming cars and where they might be in a few seconds time?' I nodded.

'From a batsman's point of view, if he is looking down at the trajectory of the spin bowler, he's in the prime position, like the person on the bridge. You see, a flat trajectory from the spinner gives the batsman every advantage. From the instant he releases the ball the batsman will know precisely where the ball will land.'

That made sense. I wasn't a good bowler out of luck, I was bowling 'flat' deliveries. No matter how accurate I was, no matter how much I turned the ball the batsman always had the upper hand. Clarrie continued: 'Now if you were so ill-advised to be standing in a manhole in the middle of that highway (please don't try this, Ashley) you would find it difficult to judge when the vehicles would reach your position because they would be above your eye line. From a batting perspective, it is the bowler who spins hard and gets the ball on a trajectory of just above the eye line who causes the batsman most problems.' Hard spun and above the batsman's eye line. Simple. Brilliant. It was my cricketing light-bulb moment. Bingo! He had a rope strung across the pitch and got me to spin hard and get the ball on a trajectory of just above the rope and on to a good length. Wow. I had finally got it.

After the session Clarrie showed me some of his cricket memorabilia, the cricket case with *Australian Cricket Team, England, 1930* emblazoned across it, the cricket ball he used to take all 10 Yorkshire wickets on that tour and myriad photographs of the man in action.

I thanked him for his time and we shook hands. He said: 'Well, young man, that will be the sum of $6.50.' I told him I would need to go to the bank before I returned for lesson number two.

'Make it tomorrow,' he said firmly.

Next day, before I returned to the Grimmett family home I took a detour to the bank. I overdrew my account to the tune of $15, for I knew another lesson would cost me at least a further $6.50 and I needed a few bob for the bus fare to my digs in Kensington.

Was it worth it? Yes, indeed.

A day or so later I received a telegram from my father in Perth. The Ayr Cricket Club had accepted my application to become the club's professional-cum-groundsman for the 1967 season. What an opportunity to try my newfound strategy.

This wasn't rocket science, just good, old-fashioned logic with a big dollop of commonsense. Undoubtedly the experience with Clarrie Grimmett was my light-bulb moment. It changed my life in so many ways. Within 18 months I was playing Test cricket, but first to cricket in Ayr.

Chapter 30

The haven Adelaide

The train lurched and slipped away. To my left was the Lion Factory, a multi-storey red-brick building, with an impressive carved stone lion atop. Self-raising and plain flour milling on site is something of the past but the carving still exists. The building is now the Lion Arts Factory, home to the Jam Factory, supporter and promoter of outstanding design and craftsmanship of global acclaim. In a few days I would be playing cricket on the other side of the world. My mind kept harking back to Clarrie Grimmett's words: 'The above-eye-line trajectory is the best lesson you'll learn about spin bowling. What you have to do is to apply it to your game. The most important thing about spin bowling is how the ball arrives ... not where it lands.'

It now all made sense to me. When I was 16 years old, I watched Richie Benaud bowling to Norm O'Neill in the nets at WACA Ground in Perth. They were training with the 1961 Australian team a few days before playing WA, then boarding the ship bound for England. As I watched from the side of the net I became fascinated by O'Neill who thrashed one ball for what would have been a scorching boundary, blocked the next three balls before unleashing another powerful cover drive. Every ball appeared the same in pace and length. So what was happening here? Oh, I concluded, O'Neill is resting between hitting fours.

I must have gone to see Clarrie for coaching two or three times before the telegram from my father arrived advising me that I had word from Ayr

Cricket Club. Now here I stood, Ayr Cricket Club's latest professional-cum-groundsman. The terms were interesting; a one-way airfare, a benefit match to compensate me for the lack of a return airfare, and £22 a week.

My Air India flight was due out on the Tuesday and on the previous Saturday I offered to mow the lawn. The machine was one of those confounded mowers that you had to wind the handle on top of the thing, clamp it down hard against the bonnet (I think that's what it is called) and then pull a cord at the side to start it. Unfortunately the handle slipped in my grasp, the ratchet snapped and my right hand was caught in the handle as it spun back like a runaway helicopter rotor blade. My right little finger was red and sore, but I didn't worry too unduly about it.

That night I had dinner with Mr and Mrs Langdon. Wally Langdon was a former WA batsman and chairman of the State selection committee. Years before he had played a fair bit of Lancashire League cricket and I hoped to get a few tips from him before I left. I told him about my trip to see Clarrie Grimmett and how I believed my bowling would improve out of sight. When it was time for me to depart, I must have winced a great deal when we shook hands. Wally insisted he drive me to the Royal Perth Hospital for treatment. The 'pinky' (on my bowling hand) was broken clean through. I never was fond of needles so I didn't press for another painkiller once five hours had elapsed and the doctor needed help to try and straighten the finger.

After my first trip in an aeroplane, from Perth, WA, to Perth, Scotland, I was picked up at the airport by Charlie Hill, an Irish-born, redheaded batsman with a kind heart and a heavy foot. It was a terrifying car trip from Perth to Ayr. Maybe he wasn't too pleased to see the new professional-cum-groundsman with his right hand in plaster. There were a few days of respite while my finger healed, so I took the time to follow through on Mum's parting words: 'Now, Ash, there are two things you must do during your time in Ayr. One, learn all you can about the Scottish bard Robert Burns and buy a kilt.'

Ayrshire was Burns' stamping ground and there was a wealth of written material about him. He was indeed a naughty boy, but boy could he write and get straight to the core of the matter. Buying a kilt was another thing. One day I found myself in the high street and eyed an impressive shop,

Burton's Outfitters, displaying all manner of tartans of clans, modern and ancient. I wandered in.

The attendant was a middle-aged man with a jolly round face.

'Can I help you?'

'I wish to buy a kilt.'

'Surname?'

'Mallett.'

The man looked at me quizzically, raised both hands in the air and said with a sigh, 'There are no McMalletts here.'

When I explained that it was imperative that I purchase a kilt the man softened and asked, 'What is your mother's maiden name?'

'West.'

It was then that the man sprang into action. He produced a thick, leather-bound book and began flipping the pages. In a few minutes he looked up. 'Ah, you are a Farquharson.' So I ordered the kilt. It would, the man said with a smile, be a garment comprising seven yards of material and be 'an absolute bargain at £44' – two weeks' wages.

I missed the first game, a 'friendly' and umpired. A good experience it was standing in the middle while snow fluttered down. I wore brown Hush Puppies®, a long white coat pulled over four long-sleeved sweaters. Soon enough I was playing. Grimmett's above the eye-line trajectory was ever on my mind and I was delighted the way it worked for me. Hard-spun deliveries in a dipping arc became my norm on those responsive pitches. The cricket was tense and combative, but the standard of the batting wasn't great. However, getting wickets regularly was something I had not enjoyed long before. In recent years I had struggled to get anyone out, so wickets at every outing did wonders for my confidence. That summer in Scotland gave me such belief I reckoned I was as good an off-spinner Australia possessed – despite my not yet having played a single first-class match.

Ayr's first win didn't happen until a few matches into the season. We were up against fierce rivals Kilmarnock in a twilight, 18-eight-ball-over affair. Ayr was knocked over for 45 and we copped many catcalls and booing as we took the field. I was standing at slip beside the skipper, Ian 'Hank' Johnstone.

Kilmarnock had reached 27 with the loss of just one wicket and I hadn't so much as bowled a ball.

'Give me a bowl, Hank, we can win this one.'

'Ach, no, you silly Aussie bastard. We don't want to show 'em what you've got until the time we meet them in a premiership match,' Hank laughed. But I insisted I bowl and Hank relented.

My first ball to the tall right-hander, Reverend Jim Aitchison, spun a mile, from way outside off stump, climbing over the Reverend's shoulder and nearly decapitating our keeper, who somehow managed to head it to the ground in front of the stumps. There was not a blade of grass on this pitch and I knew it was going to play tricks.

The boys told me that Rev. Aitchison was some player. He scored a big hundred against New Zealand in 1949 and a century against the 1956 Australians, in an attack that included Keith Miller and Ray Lindwall. Now 11 years on I was bowling to this Scottish legend of cricket and man of the cloth. I indicated to the umpire that I would bowl around the wicket, knowing that I must get my first hard-spun stock ball above the Reverend's eye line and outside the line of off-stump. It was a beauty. The angle around the wicket helped the ball go away a great deal and when it pitched the ball spun back through the huge gap between the Reverend's front pad and his bat and crashed into middle and off stumps.

Unperturbed Reverend Aitchison turned casually to the square leg umpire and said quietly: 'Did the keeper not take off the bails?' I didn't wait for the umpire's reply, telling the cheeky clergyman: 'On yer bike, sunshine!' – or words to that effect.

Amazingly, the rest of the Kilmarnock batsmen fell like ninepins. I got 6/8 and we won by two runs. We celebrated grandly.

I am told it was a good night.

In all matches, including the 'friendlies', I took 111 wickets for Ayr. Four things bring a young spinner belief – practice, practice, practice and results.

We played that benefit match. An insurance salesman turned up the day before.

'Do you wish to insure the match against rain. It's a mere £250.'

'Listen, mate, £250 is my plane ticket home.'

Hank Johnstone tried to talk me into insuring against rain, but I refused.

'I'll take my chances.'

As it turned out the day was a delight – blue skies and warm, round 24 degrees and sunny. I gathered a pretty good team to play Ian Johnstone's Ayr CC eleven. Victorian John 'General' Grant was one; WA opening bat Peter Kelly another, and ex West Indian spinner Charan Singh, his countryman Adzil Holder and South African all-rounder Eddie Fuller.

The idea was to give each batsman a chance to score at least one run. When the opposing skipper, Ian Johnstone, came in I was bowling. I decided to toss it up, higher and slower than normal. The ball left my hand hard-spun and dipping. It curved late and Hank came forward to push it wide of cover for his 'easy' single. But something went horribly wrong. The ball landed and spun back through the gate.

'Hey, Mr Umpire ... call him back. This is a benefit match. A bloke can't get out for none.'

Hank wouldn't hear about returning to the wicket. In the manner of William Wallace of old, Hank walked proudly from the battleground, shoulders back, head high. The scorebook stood with the notation: 'Johnstone bowled Mallett 0'.

Clarrie Grimmett would have loved it. He never gave anything away. A week before I left Ayr for Australia, I received a letter from WACA secretary Les Truman, asking me whether I would be returning to Perth or 'was there anything in the current rumour that I might try my hand in Adelaide?'

Upon my return to Perth from Ayr, I was undecided whether to stay in WA or go to South Australia, joining TJ at the Prospect Cricket Club. I had been included in the WA State Squad and practised at the WACA nets for three weeks before I spoke with Wally Langdon. Langdon once told me that as an off-spinner I should have been born in England. The popular theory in those days was that off-spinners were pretty much useless on the flint-hard tracks of Australia.

'Wally, what are the chances of me getting a regular game for WA this season?'

'Well, Ash, we are looking at you in a tussle with Ian Brayshaw for the all-rounder's spot.'

'Something's wrong with that assessment, Wally. I can't bat so I reckon I'll go to Adelaide.'

Adelaide beckoned. I believed that if I could get a full summer of Sheffield Shield cricket under my belt I was a real chance of getting in the Australian team for the forthcoming tour of England in the northern summer of 1968. I believed I had more chance of playing for Australia than getting a spot with the WA side were I to stay in Perth.

My old mate Terry Jenner, with Prospect Cricket Club president Len Sandford, met me at the Adelaide Railway Station. I joined Prospect and our first match was against University at the superb University Oval. Our new club was going through a boom period, winning almost every flag since 1961. Even the great Garry Sobers played a season or two at Prospect. Once, when Sobers played, some 10,000 crammed into Prospect Oval to watch arguably the greatest cricketer to play the game. I collected nine wickets for the match against University and during my spell in the first innings I couldn't help noticing another great, the greatest batsman the world had known, Sir Donald Bradman. The Don sat on the grass near a small gum tree at the southern end of the oval. I noticed that he positioned himself pretty much behind the bowler's arm. Was he there to have a look at the two new spin bowlers from the West? I hoped so, for I reckon I bowled in outstanding fashion and hoped my bowling found favour with the great man. As I recall we played the game over the weekend and next day I read that both TJ and I had been included in the SA State squad.

When I had been to Adelaide Oval with the WA Schoolboys team in 1958 we sat down to lunch in the old members' stand. It was during our game against Queensland, played on a pitch close to the old scoreboard. In those days matches were played on that pitch and another closer to the River End. Sometimes there were two games being played on the ground at the same time. I recall us seeing Sir Donald from a distance at the match. We schoolboys even spent a day at a Sheffield Shield match, SA v Victoria and I remember the brilliance of Victorian Jack Potter's off and cover driving.

It was the last season for leg-spinner Bruce Dooland, who played three Tests for Australia in the 1946–47 and 1947–48 seasons. He was unlucky for there were so many spin options about when he was at his peak. Queenslander Colin McCool and Victorian Doug Ring were the two leggies preventing Dooland winning a regular Test spot. So he did, as many others did, including the leg-spinning all-rounder Cecil Pepper, set sail for the Lancashire League and eventually county cricket in England.

Dooland spent five seasons at Nottinghamshire County Cricket Club, which brought him 748 wickets and 4492 runs. He was a tall man with a high graceful action, much like the Indian leg-spinner Anil Kumble. His strong fingers and wrist combined to gain terrific purchase on the ball, but like Kumble he tended to go the way of 'less purchase and more control'. Clarrie Grimmett taught him the flipper, which his style suited, and Scarlet's 'mystery' ball, and he, in turn, showed Richie Benaud how to bowl it.

Jack Potter was a specialist batsman, but he dabbled in bowling leg-breaks and maybe he gleaned how to bowl the flipper in that game we attended at the Adelaide Oval in the summer of 1957–58. Potter became head coach of the Australian Cricket Academy from 1988–1990 and he taught the young Shane Warne how to bowl the flipper. Wonderful how cricketers pay it forward at all levels.

My first training stint with the SA State squad was in October 1967. Carrying my kit in an overnight bag, I caught the bus into town and walked round the ground until I found the southern entrance. What a thrill: all those SA greats who had graced this ground, among them Don Bradman, Clarrie Grimmett, Vic Richardson and Clem Hill. The Adelaide Oval was the most beautiful cricket ground of my experience, even better than the Sydney Cricket Ground, where I had watched my first game. As I strolled about trying to find my way to the Adelaide Oval nets a man approached: 'Hello, son. You seem a bit lost. Can I help?' I told the bloke that I was trying to find my way to the State nets. He wanted to know all about me, 'What's your name? Where are you from? A spinner, eh? What type of spin bowling?'

I didn't think much of it until the next day I read an article by Ray Barber, cricket writer for the *News*, then Adelaide's afternoon tabloid newspaper:

'Mallett not being able to find his way to practice, might find his way in the SA eleven when the side is picked to play Victoria on Saturday.'

Just as I was about to move into the net area I felt a hand on my shoulder. As I turned a man in a neat, grey suit extended his right hand and said: 'Don Bradman's my name. Welcome to Adelaide and the State squad. If there is anything I can do for you, Ashley, please don't hesitate to contact me.'

Apparently TJ and I bowled well and created quite an impression at the nets. SA was lacking in spin bowling talent and happily we were both included in the State 12 for the match against Victoria. As it turned out TJ was picked in the 11 and I was made 12th man. Two days before the following Shield match I dislocated my middle finger when Alan Shiell smacked me a return catch and I not only spilt the hot chance but ruled myself out of a chance to play against NSW.

Sir Donald offered to drive me to the home of Dr Donald Beard, the SACA's 'resident' doctor. SA captain Les Favell yelled: 'Don't forget to remove your spikes before you get into Sir Donald's car!' The Don laughed and that began a relationship of sorts for few of the SA players were game enough to approach the man. I never had that problem. When The Don walked into the SA dressing room, as he did every morning of a four-day match to enjoy a cup of tea, the blokes tended to slip out into the viewing area. I stayed to speak with him. There was always the potential for a useful tip or two.

One morning I was there in the room as usual and one other player, Greg Chappell, was standing holding a bat. Sir Donald paused as he was about to leave the room and said to Greg: 'I'd change my grip if I were you, son.' For the first time in his life Greg was lost for words. Bradman picked up Greg's bat and said: 'This was my grip and it worked for me.' He then played a shadow drive. Sir Donald was then 59 years of age, yet the bat speed he could manage was remarkable. His shadow drive was so swift you couldn't see the bat clearly, it was a blur, much like the propeller of an aeroplane. I thought my eyes were playing tricks, but no. His second shadow drive was exactly the same. Greg took Sir Donald's advice.

When my finger mended I again made contact with Clarrie Grimmett to arrange for another coaching lesson. Greg Chappell and TJ came along to meet Clarrie and TJ was, like me, a sponge soaking up as much wisdom as we could from the old man. Greg too was fascinated by Clarrie's passion about spin bowling.

'Clarrie took you out to the cricket pitch and had you bowl to him. My recollection is that he was not too complimentary,' Greg recalled.

On this occasion he didn't face us with his Jack Hobbs autograph bat. He had erected a couple of tall poles and a rope was stretched – from the top of one pole to the other – across the breadth of the pitch. A whitewash rectangle with a vertical line splitting the rectangle in two equal-sized parts was drawn on a good length.

'Now, lads. The idea is for you to spin the ball up over the rope stretched across the pitch, land in one of the squares and hit the solitary stump,' Clarrie said with a smile.

'Terry, you must go over the rope and land in the right-hand square and spin your leg-break to hit the stump. You know at my peak I could land there with the leg-break and hit the stump; then my top-spinner hit the centre vertical line and went on to hit the stump and my bosey spun back from the left-hand square to hit the one stump.'

TJ and I made eye contact.

Greg Chappell took up the story:

I can't remember his exact language, but it was all about bowling the ball and getting it above the batsman's eye line so that the batsman had to work harder to calculate length and drop. I became aware of a noticeable difference in your bowling from that time. You appeared to get up and over the ball a lot better so drift and drop increased, which added a layer to the challenge of batting against you. Interestingly, you appeared to stand taller at the point of release from that time so you got full advantage of your height and long prehensile fingers.

The greatest impression Grimmett made on us that day was the idea of spinning up, above the eye line of the batsman. Years later when we became spin bowling coaches, that lesson was always central to our philosophy on spin bowling. We simply paid forward what Clarrie Grimmett had taught us. TJ became Shane Warne's mentor when the young spinner was at the Adelaide Cricket Academy during Rod Marsh's tenure as head coach.

Like his mentor TJ, Warne was a sponge. He soaked it all up. TJ said Warney never took as gospel any new idea or addition to his repertoire he suggested without first thinking long and hard about it, trying it in the nets and getting the feel of it.

'Sometimes he went with it, sometimes not,' TJ said. 'Shane had the gift of being able to achieve remarkable spin on the ball. I was always fascinated watching the youngster pick up a ball and hear it fizz through the air as he spun it from right hand to left. You can't teach that: it's a God-given gift.'

That first summer of 1967–68 saw me bowl impressively for SA and I was picked in the Australian team bound for England. Sir Donald Bradman, Chairman of the Australian selection committee, congratulated me on being picked then promptly told me I had to add two paces to my run up. I guess he believed that a longer approach might help me get more energy through the crease. I added two paces – from five to seven – to my run up.

Long ago in Adelaide Grimmett discovered the magic of spin; later so too did Bruce Dooland, David Sincock, TJ, Tim May, Nathan Lyon and me.

It was A.G. 'Johnny' Moyes who wrote: 'Adelaide, the haven for unwanted bowlers and the staging post for England.' Yes, indeed. A haven and a staging post.

Clarrie Grimmett's influence and advice was immense. The Grimmett philosophy had already influenced generations of leg-spinners. At the age of 10, Richie Benaud saw Grimmett get two wickets with his new 'mystery' ball, the flipper, for SA versus NSW at the SCG. The year was 1940, and it was one of the last matches Grimmett played. His final first-class wicket was Arthur Morris. Many years later Grimmett's influence indirectly had a profound impact on the great Shane Warne. But that came much later.

Right now my real adventure was about to start.

Chapter 31

The Oval: my spiritual home

The cricket gods smiled on me that August day at The Oval in 1968, my Test debut. With the fifth ball of my first over I claimed the wicket of Colin Cowdrey. In a game against Surrey a few weeks earlier, Australian-born umpire Cec Pepper made it known he didn't like my constant appeals. 'Rowdy,' he said sternly, 'you'll never die wondering.' In that first Test match over I asked the question four times. As the fifth ball left my hand I knew it was a rip-snorter. It developed a lovely curve and dipped menacingly in flight before breaking back sharply to trap the Kipper dead in front. Umpire Charlie Elliott raised his finger and Cowdrey looked up, touched the peak of his cap and said politely, 'Well bowled, master.'

Before I moved from Perth to Adelaide to get a game, I was a sometimes member of the Limp Fall Club, a global institution inspired by its founder, the great cartoonist Paul Rigby. At Australia's team meeting at the Waldorf Hotel the night before the Test, the instant I realised I was in the XI, I celebrated in true limp fall tradition, throwing myself backwards off my chair and hitting my head on the fireplace. A sore head, yes, but nothing would prevent me playing that first Test match (although the incident ended my limp fall career). I picked up five wickets for the match and was delighted that I could hold up against the strong England batting line-up, which included luminaries such as Ted Dexter, Tom Graveney, Basil D'Oliveira, Colin Milburn and John Edrich. England scored 494, with D'Oliveira hitting a career-best 158. Australia was 237 for 7 when I joined Bill Lawry. We survived to stumps.

The next day we stood together for two minutes in silent respect for Stan McCabe, who had died tragically at his Sydney home the previous day. When his score had reached 135 and our partnership 32, Lawry was given out caught behind. The umpire, Arthur Fagg, obviously didn't see what I saw, for the ball nipped back from outside off, clipped Lawry high on the back leg and flew through to the keeper. The Phantom was not amused. I batted for three hours and hit what turned out to be my highest Test score, 43 not out, and somehow we avoided the follow-on. An old Aussie Digger, A.J. Kirk, wrote me a lovely letter, praising my innings and fight. He mistakenly likened it to the battle he fought as a young man at Gallipoli. But I knew that cricket is just a game: war is hell.

Rain came, but not enough for our liking. There was the unforgettable image of the rotund Cowdrey, resplendent in creams and England blazer, standing under a brolly in the middle of the ground near two large puddles of water. As Cowdrey surveyed the scene, the ground announcer told spectators that anyone who helped mop up the water would receive a payment of 12 shillings and sixpence. The ground was cleared in no time and the Australians fell like a pack of cards. Derek Underwood ran amok, claiming 7/50. On an uneven or wet surface Underwood was indeed 'Deadly'.

In 1972 Australia had to win the fifth Test, at The Oval, to square the series. The wicket was hard and fast, very much like Brisbane. It provided bounce and carry for the quick bowlers and ample turn and bounce for the spinners. Dennis Lillee bowled quite magnificently, taking 5/58, and to my joy I bowled a lot in tandem with him and picked up 3/80 off 23 overs. I particularly liked getting rid of Tony Greig, caught at slip by Keith Stackpole, with a ball that curved away from the bat and bounced to take an outside edge. England scored a moderate 284, with Alan Knott, that serial pest of a batsman, hitting 92. He had a funny front-on stance, holding the bat as if he were playing French cricket.

Rarely would Knott launch into a drive, but he could whip to leg, cut along the ground or over the slips, and deflect the ball hockey-style either side of the wicket. A brilliant 201 partnership for the third wicket by the

Chappell brothers (Ian 118 and Greg 113) saw Australia reach a total of 399. I was run out for 5 and the instant I set foot in the dressing room my captain said with a smile: 'Didn't you want us to reach 400, Rowd?'

Batting a second time England got 356: Barry Wood hooked brilliantly for 90, helped by a string of moderate scores. That pest Knott belted a quickfire 63 before Lillee knocked his middle stump back to grab 5/123. I took 2/66 and we needed 242 to win. The pitch had not slowed a lot, but there were rough patches and the dust flew when Ian Chappell advanced down the track to drive the spin of Ray Illingworth. Rod Marsh and Paul Sheahan got us home with an unbeaten sixth-wicket stand of 71. The pair ran off the ground in jubilation, Marsh madly waving his bat. In the after-match celebration Marsh stood on a chair and sang his rendition of what became our official team song. He apparently adapted the lyrics from a well-known poem about a sprig of wattle.

My last Test at The Oval was in 1975. It was a dull and boring affair on a wicket that was as lifeless as a dead dingo. The England players were on the front foot to Jeff Thomson, a ploy that only a few months previously would have proved fatal on the lightning-fast Perth track.

The Oval is famous for its gas holders, which have towered near the ground since 1861, seven years before W.G. Grace turned up to watch the 1868 Aboriginal team play Surrey. During a break in play in that match, the Aboriginals delighted the crowd with demonstrations of their skill in hurling spears and boomerangs. The 20-year-old Grace, then a spitting image of Ned Kelly, made the fans sit up by throwing a cricket ball 118 yards one way, then 109 yards against the wind. In 1882 at The Oval, Australia won for the first time in England, thus spawning The Ashes legend. Walking onto The Oval in a Test match is very special to Test players because you are following in the footsteps of the greats: Grace, Trumper, Bradman, Hobbs, O'Reilly, Hutton, Laker. I think fondly of England, its people, their humour, the lovely tone of their voices north and south, and their pride in the summer game. In a cricket sense I consider The Oval to be my spiritual home.

Chapter 32

Bradman versus Warne

Having lived through the epic Shane Warne–Sachin Tendulkar contests – the master batsman of the age versus the champion batsman – I have always wondered how Bradman would have dealt with the sublime spin of Warne. O how I wish Albert Einstein realised that things could go faster than light and a time machine was potential reality.

However, in the absence of a time machine we can use our imagination. We can look at old footage of Bradman and film of Warne; we can research and analyse and use part of the 95 per cent of the human mind we usually don't utilise and come up with the unimaginable: a contest between Bradman and Warne. Sometimes the unreal melds with the real, but fantasy is fantasy; or is it? Imagine such a contest.

As the hand on the clock struck the hour, fans in their thousands pour into the Melbourne Cricket Ground to witness first-hand the greatest cricket battle of them all: Bradman versus Warne. Sid Barnes, stalwart of the 1948 *Invincibles* and Arthur Morris' opening partner, falls to Shane Warne's second ball, a hard-spun leg-break which left his hand and curved down the pitch in a lovely arc to send Banjo Paterson into his own poetic 'Song of Spin'.

As Barnes probes forward, the hissing Warne leg-break ducks swiftly, like a diving Spitfire, and the batsman's failure to cover neither the length nor the breadth of spin, presents Mark Taylor with a dolly at first slip. Already

THWACK!

100,000 people have packed the MCG and they rise as one to give the greatest batsman of all time the most magnificent reception. Taylor sidles up to Warne. They have a brief chat as they watch Bradman walk briskly to centre stage.

'Well, Tubs, this could be quite something if I can get him to take the bait.'

Taylor's smile says it all. He pats his champion leggie on the shoulder and heads back to slip, making sure Jason Gillespie is in nice and close at mid-on. Bradman's trademark single off the mark is invariably a run just wide of mid-on. Barnes tries in vain to mention to Bradman that the ball is dipping wickedly and that the leg-spin magician has the ball on a string. The Don is in no mood to talk to anyone about the merits of a bowler for whom he has great respect, but a man he dearly wants to thrash unmercifully.

On the 1930 Australian tour of England the brash 20-year-old batting phenomenon told his teammates, 'Plenty of batsmen watch the bowler's fingers hoping to detect what sort of ball he's going to deliver, but that's no good to me. Let me see the ball coming and then I'll decide the best place to hit it.' Never would he stop on his way to the wicket to hear the outgoing batsman describe how much the ball is swinging (were the bowler a medium pacer), or the turn and bounce being achieved by a spinner.

Maybe Clarrie Grimmett, the greatest slow leg-spinner between the wars, told him of the Test trial at the SCG in 1925 when Grimmett spun one a good deal to trap Tommy Andrews. Grimmett watched the departing batsman and saw how he stopped to chat to the man next in, Alan Kippax. There was Andrews demonstrating with arms outstretched how the ball that got him 'spun a mile'. Kippax lasted one ball: a fizzing Grimmett top-spinner ripped between bat and pad to hit middle stump as Kippax played with his bat away from the pad to counter what he expected, 'excessive turn'.

So the stage is set. Taylor remembers how Sachin Tendulkar attacked Warne in India and succeeded with big hundreds in three innings. Will Bradman go at Warne in a similar vein? Bradman takes guard, looks about the field, and takes up his stance. Warne has a slip, backward point, short cover, extra cover and mid-off.

To the on side is a man behind square leg, a very straight mid-wicket, mid-on and a man in the deep just in front of square. The crowd falls silent. They know that this contest will provide something very special, for both players are at the pinnacle of their powers.

When the world thought that the art of leg-spin had disappeared forever like the dinosaurs, who failed to duck a barrage of cosmic bouncers, Warne turned up to charm the cricket world with his magnificent slow bowling. He never got the chance to bowl to Victor Trumper, the one regarded to be the greatest batsman of the Golden Age of Cricket. That would have been fascination enough, for Trumper batted to entertain. Mostly he was satisfied with a century and then he'd look about the field for the most 'deserving bowler' and promptly give that man his wicket. He averaged just 39 in 48 Tests, but he played all of his cricket on uncovered wickets. When rain, wind and sun set to work on such a wicket in Australia it usually resulted in what the old timers called a 'sticky dog'. On such a treacherous track at the MCG in January 1904, Trumper hit 74 out of 122. His display was hailed as a miracle innings because the instant most of Wilfred Rhodes' deliveries hit the surface of the wicket the ball rose like a striking cobra: bringing sudden death to an array of good players including Reg Duff, Clem Hill, Monty Noble, Syd Gregory and Warwick Armstrong. Trumper batted as if there wasn't a gremlin to be seen, just as Bradman was expected to bat against any bowler of any generation.

But today it is all about Bradman and Warne. Bradman was totally ruthless. He was said to have targeted bowlers, setting out to destroy them on the field. Once in a grade match in Adelaide he went to the wicket late on a Saturday afternoon. The light was fading and the big fast bowler standing at mid-on might ruffle the champion's feathers if he bowled fast next over on the green track in bad light. The Don hit all eight deliveries of the bowler's over just out of reach of the big quick at mid-on. By the time the over ended and he was expected to bowl to Bradman, the poor man was so exhausted he couldn't scratch himself.

In the late 1990s, Bradman said of Warne, that he was 'the best thing to happen to Australian cricket in 30 years'. Round that time Sir Donald invited Sachin Tendulkar and Shane Warne to his Kensington Park home in Adelaide. It was a pleasant change from having busloads of people – even

Japanese tourists – turn up unannounced to snap their cameras in a frenzy of celebrity worship towards this perky little champion who, because of his extraordinary skill with a cricket bat, was given a life sentence as a prisoner of fame.

At the age of 16, Len Hutton faced 62-year-old S.F. Barnes in the nets and years later he declared that Barnes 'was the best bowler I've faced'. Bradman considered Bill O'Reilly to be the greatest bowler he had played with or against.

Sir Donald wrote me in 1989:

> Of all the bowlers I played with and against I rate Bill O'Reilly No. 1. In my opinion the hardest ball to play is the one which turns from leg to off and this was Bill's stock delivery. He persistently bowled at a right-hander's leg-stump and when perfectly pitched that ball would take the off bail. There is precious little answer to such a delivery – the batsman actually gets an outside edge or the ball clips the off-stump. Bill also bowled a magnificent bosey (wrong-un or googly) which was hard to pick and which he aimed at middle and leg stumps. It was fractionally slower than his leg-break and usually dropped a little in flight and 'sat up' to entice a catch to one of his two short-leg fieldsmen. These two deliveries, combined with great accuracy and unrelenting hostility, were enough to test the greatest of batsmen, particularly as his leg-break was bowled at medium pace – quicker than the normal run of slow bowlers – thereby making it extremely difficult for a batsman to use his feet as a counter measure. Bill will always remain in my book, the greatest of all.

(Don Bradman letter to A. Mallett, 5 May 1989)

O'Reilly dined with S.F. Barnes at a London restaurant in 1934 and Bill asked S.F., who also medium-paced leg-breaks, where he placed his short legs for his wrong'un.

'Don't need one,' he said bluntly.

How did Bradman rate Clarrie Grimmett, O'Reilly's great spinning partner?

> I always classified Clarrie as the best of the genuine slow leg-spinners (I exclude O'Reilly because, as you say, he was not really a slow leggie) and what made him the best was his accuracy. His control was remarkable. I saw

Clarrie in one match take the ball after some light rain when the ball was greasy and hard to hold yet he reeled off five maidens without a loose ball. That is the problem with young leg-break bowlers – it takes years to develop such control and in the meantime they are too expensive and get discarded.

(Don Bradman letter to A. Mallett, 1 March 1991)

As far as I know Sir Donald never aired in public any comparison of Grimmett with Warne.

Perhaps Warne's emergence was too late in Bradman's life to make such comparisons, for invariably it would have led to his being hounded by the press. Who'd want that as you enter your nineties?

So today Bradman will learn about Warne's greatness.

Bradman again looks about the field. Warne has Taylor at slip, Matthew Hayden at backward point, Ricky Ponting at short cover, Mark Waugh at extra cover and Steve Waugh at mid-off. As the keeper Ian Healy settles down with a 'Carn, Shane', Merv Hughes moves in at backward square leg; so too does David Boon at short straight mid-wicket and Jason Gillespie at mid-on. At deep square leg Glenn McGrath ambles in a few yards.

There is a hush in the crowd. Mark Nicholas says in his quiet authoritative tone: 'Well, now, the stage is set ... the greatest batsman of all time about to meet the greatest bowler of the ages.'

Warne stands at the top of his mark. His spinning fingers move a little up and down as he caresses the ball, ensuring the grip is neither too loose nor too tight, but firm. Bradman's eyes are set on the blond leg-spinner. When the camera zooms in for a close-up, TV viewers are looking at a man totally focused; a man on a mission.

All eyes turn to Warne as he starts his methodical way to the wicket. When he gets within a yard of the crease his wrist cocks and he drives up and over his front leg with amazing energy and strength. The ball spins so hard it hums, dipping in a lovely curve with the trajectory of an archer's arrow. Bradman can't hit this one for six, four, three, two or one, so he goes well forward and meets the ball with a dead bat.

No run.

Warne stands at the end of his follow through and rubs his chin. Bradman avoids his stare, looking about the field. He sees gaps on the on side, but knows all too well that hitting those gaps will be risky against hard spun leg-breaks which, if Warne's on song, will arrive in a fizzing, dipping arc.

Warne again. A leg-break. It curves in towards leg-stump and upon pitching it fairly buzzes, spinning past Bradman's forward defensive stroke. The ball misses off by a whisker and as the crowd roars in appreciation of the bowler's skill, Healy takes it, throwing his head back.

Ball three arrives, again dipping menacingly in a lovely curve. Don Bradman pounces with feline reflexes, his feet moving swiftly, yet with silky smoothness to reach the ball the instant it strikes the turf. There can be no error, for to misjudge the length would be fatal. Bradman pounces like a cat nailing a mouse and his cover drive scorches past Ponting at short cover, beats Mark Waugh at extra and scuttles like a startled rabbit to the boundary. The enthralling battle goes for an hour. Bradman has scored freely up the other end and has taken about a dozen runs off Warne. Two boundaries and four singles. In the meantime Arthur Morris, who was Clarrie Grimmett's last first-class wicket, falls to Glenn McGrath, and Lindsay Hassett, one of the few batsmen to repeatedly play well against O'Reilly, proves a good ally for Bradman and a big partnership looms.

But Warne has other ideas. He has used his full repertoire: the leg-break, fizzing top-spinner, back-spinner, zooter, wrong'un and flipper. Just one wrong'un to Bradman, which he latched on to as he so often did when Grimmett bowled that ball. Bradman always said Grimmett's wrong'un was easy to pick and he found that with Warne. His flipper too made little impact.

Bradman was alert to that ball which Grimmett had invented and Warne bowled so well to many, especially the South African Daryll Cullinan, who once told me he always 'picked' Warne's flipper, but, alas, kept getting bowled by it.

Some 75 minutes into the match, the Invincibles score stands at 2/94: Bradman 49 and Hassett 17. Warne decides to go back to total reliance on his stock ball. He will concentrate, as he always did early in a spell, to bowl hard-spun leg-breaks and vary, ever so slightly, the pace of those deliveries. Bradman has batted with assurance and skill but he has found Warne's bowling to be an extraordinary mix of O'Reilly and Grimmett wrapped up in one amazing bowler. Warne has the spin and the guile of Grimmett, in fact, he spins harder and the ball drops more dramatically than the man they called 'Scarlet' and he also possesses O'Reilly's 'unrelenting hostility'.

Warne moves in again. He bowls a hard-spun leg-break, but this time with a slight, almost imperceptible change of pace. One-hundred-thousand people watching at the ground, plus millions on television, are fooled. So too is Don Bradman.

Although Bradman's footwork is swift and sure, the ball dips suddenly and wickedly and lands well short of where The Don expects. Too far into his stroke to check it, his lofted drive goes straight into the sure hands of Ponting at short cover.

Bradman c. Ponting b. Warne 49.

Chapter 33

Best little Test match ground in Australasia

The cricketing gods have their favourites – players such as Victor Trumper, Don Bradman, Sachin Tendulkar and Shane Warne spring to mind. They also have their favourite Test match grounds. Unquestionably Wellington's iconic Basin Reserve is a favourite among the gods. Why else would they have conspired to cut the ever-biting and howling Wellington wind and flood the Basin with sunshine for the whole of the 2014 Test match between NZ and India? This was a special game for they knew Brendon McCullum was about to explode with a triple century (he finished with 302) and there was also the mouth-watering prospect of watching the glorious stroke play of India's Virat Kohli. The game ended in a tame draw, but how the Wellington fans lapped up five sun-drenched days without a breath of wind.

In 1840, when the first settlers arrived, the ground as we know today was covered by water. It was a shallow lagoon, and not until the 1855 earthquake did the ground rise sufficiently for it to become a swamp. In 1863 prisoners were put to good use helping drain the swamp. By 1866, the Basin Reserve became the home of Cricket Wellington. Situated two kilometres from the heart of the city, the Basin lies at the foot of Mount Victoria. Government House and Wellington College Boys' School are south of the Basin, across the street mostly hidden behind a stand of majestic old trees.

The Basin has the feel of a quaint English cricket ground. There is seating under cover, but also a lovely stretch of undulating hill, so spectators have the best of both worlds. Before the 1855 Wairarapa earthquake, which lifted the area by 1.8 metres, the city fathers had plans to connect the lagoon (known as the Basin Lake) to the sea, creating an alternative inner-city harbour. The plans included architect's drawings for warehouses and factories running along its edge.

My first visit to The Basin was with Ian Chappell's side in 1974. In those days the old grandstand doubled as the teams' dressing rooms and luncheon pavilion. It has since been transformed (well, the ground floor) into a museum and is well worth a visit if you're going to the cricket for a day's play. There is something very calming, old worlde, even gentle about the Basin. In 1974 the wicket ran parallel to Mount Victoria and the grandstand. In that Test match the wind howled as if it had been
sent straight from Antarctica. Despite the wind-chill factor, which turned the bowlers' fingers blue, there were no such worries for the batsmen. In a thoroughly run-soaked affair the Chappell brothers Ian (145 and 121) and Greg (247 not out and 133) dominated proceedings, although in the wake of NZ hitting 484 there was no time to somehow force a result.

In the late 1890s Clarrie Grimmett, the little NZ-born leg-spinner, who won fame as a bowler for Australia between the wars after leaving his native land, used to slip down to the Basin with a shovel in a hand and the two Harris brothers who lived next door in nearby Roxburgh Street in tow to play their impromptu games of cricket. The outfield was rough but a little 'gardening' with shovel and feet and the boys soon fashioned a piece of ground worthy of a Test match at the Basin. This boutique ground has the charm of Worcester's county ground at New Road. It couldn't cater for a crowd in excess of 10,000 but for the cricket purist crowd numbers matter not a stolen chip by an alert seagull. Grimmett played a couple of first-class games for Wellington on the Basin in 1911. Three years later, in 1914, he turned out for Wellington against an Australian XI, which included such luminaries as Victor Trumper and Warwick Armstrong. The Australian XI was brought to Wellington by Test leg-spinner Arthur Mailey.

Clarrie's greatest thrill was to bowl to his hero Victor Trumper. 'It was a great moment for me,' Clarrie told me when I visited his home in Adelaide in 1967 – 53 years later.

'Trumper took two runs off my over, and he showed lots of respect for my efforts. Sadly he got out the other end next over and that was the only time I bowled to him. I always regretted that, but I was glad to have had the chance to bowl to that greatest of batsmen.'

During the lunchbreak on the first day of the first match, several of the Australian players indicated to the Wellington players that they would be only too happy to 'give us any hints they could and they urged us not to be backward in asking'.

In 1914 Clarrie could bowl the leg-break and the bosey (wrong'un) with equal accuracy. His length or direction did not suffer, whichever ball he decided to deliver. However, Clarrie was interested to find out just how the great leg-spinner Arthur Mailey went about bowling the bosey (wrong'un).

'Mr Mailey, could you please show me how you bowl the bosey?'

Without so much as a word to young Grimmett, Mailey picked up the ball, ran leisurely into the empty net and delivered a nicely spun bosey which, upon pitching, turned, as intended, appreciably from the off.

'This did not convey very much,' Clarrie said, 'so I asked Mailey if he wouldn't mind showing me how he bowled the ball again.'

Mailey didn't say a word. He sauntered in, bowled another bosey, then walked away. The young Grimmett was livid. The Mailey snub to an emerging New Zealand cricketer belied his image as an entertainer and a man with a keen sense of humour. That was the start of a keen rivalry between the established Mailey and the up-and-coming Grimmett in Australian cricket.

After much trial and tribulation trying to make his name as a spinner in Sydney, then Melbourne and finally in Adelaide, Grimmett was picked for the last Ashes Test of the 1924–25 summer. He was then aged 33 and a man that age needed to make an impact straightaway in Australian cricket.

Impact indeed. Grimmett took 5/45 in England's first innings and 6/37 when they batted again: a total of 31.3 overs for a match haul of 11/82. His spin bowling partner in that game, Arthur Mailey, bowled just five overs for the game and a return of 0/13. It wasn't long before Grimmett took over from Mailey and forged a great spin bowling liaison with Bill O'Reilly – the Tiger and the Fox. And it all began for Grimmett at Wellington's Basin Reserve.

Wellington is a thriving little harbour town. Curiously and thankfully there is precious little graffiti to be seen in the downtown area itself, and in and about the docks the people embrace the opportunity to stroll, power walk, jog or cycle the impressive wide walkways by the water. The Adelaide Oval was once the grand old Colonial cricket ground of the nation. Now the ground has been transformed into a modern facility, which outstrips any big stadium in the land. The famous old scoreboard (built in the year of Clarrie Grimmett's debut first-class match) remains, but it is not as it was: some say the oval has lost its soul; others praise it as a far better outfitted modern sports ground, more comfortable: a brilliant sports venue for the new era.

All that tells this writer that Wellington's Basin Reserve is now unquestionably the the best boutique Test match ground in Australasia.

Chapter 34

'Rice bowls and Paddy fields'

Famous lyricist, writer and poet Sir Tim Rice has an unbridled passion for cricket. The final Australia–England match at The Oval in 1953 became the all-important Ashes-deciding match for eight-year-old Tim Rice all set to watch the game from the family lounge room. Television itself had been fast-tracked to British life, courtesy of the BBC's live telecast of the Coronation of Queen Elizabeth two months earlier.

'I was hooked for life after the 1953 Test match,' Tim told me as we sat in the comfy confines of the spacious foyer of Adelaide's Intercontinental Hotel a year or so ago. 'I became a cricket junkie and absorbed the facts and figures, characters and culture of this great game with the thoroughness and fanaticism with which I had taken up astronomy three years earlier.

'When I set eyes on a copy of the 1954 *Wisden* (the cricketers' bible) I felt pretty much as I suspect Keats did on his first reading of Chapman's *Homer*,' Tim smiled.

'Cricket pushed all other interests to the sidelines, although I do remember being thrilled by the eclipse of the sun in 1954,' he wrote in his highly entertaining autobiography *Oh, What a Circus* (Hodder & Stoughton, London, 1999). 1

During his formative years at Popefield Farm, Tim and his brothers Jo and Andy found they spent as much time in and about the 17th and 18th century barns as they did in their bedrooms. He noted that the area was pretty much fauna free courtesy of a few cows wandering about, the odd rat and a 'psychopath of a barn cat'. The garden became the favourite playground for tame cats, chickens, hamsters, white rabbits and a boxer, which, like Hitler, only had one ball, they named Prinz 'in deference to the breed's German origins'. 'Both the acquisition of this adorable hound and several of the au pair girls who were part of the household in the fifties demonstrated that my parents were free from any post-war Teutonic hangover.'

Stamp collecting was one of Tim's early joys and the activity proved to be his first introduction to a pretty young woman called Eva Peron who was featured on all the Argentinian stamps. It wasn't just collecting the stamps, Tim became a young philatelist and the study of Eva Peron later led to the wonderful stage production, *Evita*.

Tim, Jo and Andy were always engaged in Test matches at their Popefield Farm home. They invented a form of cricket they called 'Sloggers'. The family farmhouse was surrounded by old barns. The brothers used a tennis ball and a hit to the stone wall was four; a hit past the stone wall to barn door on the full was six, a hit to a barn roof was eight and to somehow lob a ball on to the flat-roofed chicken house was a 12. Their own rules were roughly based on the odd rules devised by the boys at Eton College in the 17th and 18th centuries, whereupon they played a handball game called Eton Fives, in a confined area between a stone wall and a couple of buttresses on the side of Eton College Chapel. As at Eton, the Rice boys found their own way of playing a form of ball game whereby scoring was of their own invention and pretty much captive to their environment. A decent hit over the barn roof was instant dismissal so it required clever timing to find the little chicken-house rooftop to register a 12.

Tim always reckoned his brother, Jo, now the Kent County Cricket Club chairman, had more ability than he, however, he still recalls, with pride, his 208 against Jo's bowling in 1956.

England won that famous 1953 Test match at The Oval due mainly to the spinning exploits of Jim Laker and Tony Lock. However, the left-arm wrist spin of Johnny Wardle (Yorkshire) and Denis Compton (Middlesex), both England Test players, were the two slow men who best inspired his bowling.

'In the summer of 1957 I, very briefly, thought I might be a competent cricketer and found I could bowl quite accurate slow left arm stuff, a la

Johnny Wardle (20 Tests, 102 wickets at an average of 20.39),' Rice said in his autobiography. 'I batted and bowled left-handed, which was strange because I never did anything else in life that way round.' But the cricket fell away and Tim spent most of his school sports time in the swimming pool.

Tim's father, Hugh Gordon Rice, served in the Eighth Army during WWII and reached the rank of major. His mother Joan Odette (nee Bawden) served in the Women's Auxiliary Air Force (WAAF) as a photographic interpreter. When Hugh Rice first set eyes on baby Tim he described him thus: 'Fine and hearty but I was a bit apprehensive of something so small and of such an odd colour. He weighed 8 lbs 6 oz and had little wispy hair.'

Years later Tim remarked: 'Not the best, but certainly not the worst, review I was to get in my life.'

Eight years later Tim's father Hugh was appointed Far East representative for de Havilland which meant lengthy stints away in places such as Hong Kong, Japan and Singapore. Hugh's main job at the time was to sell de Havilland's new star performer, the *DH Comet*. The boys recognised how tough their father's long absences had been on their mother, as 'quick flips to the other end of the globe were out of the question in those days'. Hugh Rice even missed one Christmas which 'went down like a Mexican wave at a funeral'.

In 1955 Hugh was asked to spend a full year in Japan to restore the Far Eastern buyers' confidence in the troubled Comet. Tim reckoned his father would have resigned had he not been able to take his family with him. The journey to Japan on the *Bayernstein*, a German vessel on its first voyage, was an education in itself for the six weeks at sea were spent swimming every day and getting much better than his former self as a dog paddler and learning about foreign currency. All the transactions aboard ship were in marks and pfennigs and 'for the only time in my life I was an advocate for decimalisation'. While his father fought to win the Asia Pacific region confidence in the Comet, Tim greatly improved his swimming with daily plunges in Tokyo's American Club Pool.

Tim attended St Mary's International school in Tokyo, run by an order of Canadian monks, the Brothers of Christian Instruction. Tim said in *Oh, What a Circus*:

I suppose I became slightly religious as a result of the Brothers' force-feeding. I used to recite the occasional Hail Mary out of school and became fascinated with the words of the Lord's Prayer, for language reasons as well as for religious ones. I said my prayers every night, asking God to forgive me and bless my family and friends. But I was pretty low-key about it.

After nine months of great experience in a young boy's life, the Rice family headed home. Hugh Rice had meetings in a variety of Asian cities and the family flew all the way. Two years earlier Tim had first experienced air travel, when he accompanied his father to an air show in Kent. The aircraft, a *DH Dove*, took off from the de Havilland runway, a huge area, an important part of the Rice family's backyard. The return journey from Japan had their aircraft stop briefly at an impressive array of exotic places – Burma, India, Thailand and Pakistan.

'I tended to judge each place by the quality of their swimming pools, but, as had been the case during the whole fantastic nine months, I was just about old and aware enough to know that this could be as good as it gets,' states Rice in his autobiography.

By the time the family returned to the UK and he once again attended Aldwickbury, Tim Rice discovered, to his delight, that he was the best swimmer in the school. Eventually, thanks to Tim's father, the *Comet* flew again in 1955 and was reintroduced to commercial service in 1958. The Rice family returned to the UK from Japan in 1956. That summer Hugh Rice took Tim to Lord's to watch his first match (Middlesex versus Sussex) live.

Two of Tim's favourite players were Denis Compton and Bill Edrich, although he was too young to have seen their batting exploits in the glorious summer of 1947. That season Middlesex won the county championship due mostly to Compton (3816 runs at 90.85) and Edrich (3539 runs at 80.43).

While not considering himself an intellectual, by the age of six or seven Tim had read a lot of children's classics such as *Alice in Wonderland, Treasure Island* and 'the wonderful works of E. Nesbit – and I loved the nonsense poetry of Edward Lear'. By the mid 50s Tim's favourite reading included the popular comic the *Eagle*, newspapers and, of course, *Wisden*.

By the time Tim was ten years old he had become fascinated by the cinema. Animation, especially, took his fancy. He saw most of the Disney classic full-length features such as *Peter Pan* and *Dumbo* and he loved Tom and Jerry, Bugs Bunny, Tweety and Sylvester – 'indeed, almost anything in cartoon form'. Some 40 years later and the early cartoon experience stood Tim in good stead for his work for the Disney Studios on *The Lion King* and *Aladdin*.

Tim started 'writing silly poems' at an early age, but it never occurred to him that he would one day be a writer. 'At school the head boys used "writing essays" as punishment and it soon became my constant "punishment" because they found then "funny".'

Wednesday 21 April 1965 turned out to be a significant day in the life of Tim Rice. That was the day he sat down and wrote a short letter to a young man he had never met, a young man recommended to him by a book publisher. Tim thought he and this chap, Andrew Lloyd Webber, might be able to write some songs together. Tim was 21 and Andrew just 17. Tim Rice never baulked at Andrew Lloyd Webber's 'insane suggestion that I become the Hammerstein to his Rodgers'.

He did not seek a university place, but spent a year studying at the Sorbonne in Paris. After this, Rice joined EMI Records as a management trainee in 1966. But the meeting with Andrew Lloyd Webber a year earlier lit the flame in what would become an extraordinary collaboration of magic minds and music. 'With Andrew (Lloyd Webber) it was always a joint effort', Tim wrote.

Tim Rice is best known for his collaborations with Andrew Lloyd Webber, with whom he wrote *Joseph and the Amazing Technicolor Coat*, *Jesus Christ Superstar* and *Evita*. He also collaborated with Björn Ulvaeus and Benny Andersson of ABBA, with whom he wrote *Chess*. He wrote additional songs for the 2011 West End revival of *The Wizard of Oz*. Tim also wrote all the songs in his work alongside Alan Menken in the globally acclaimed musical *Aladdin*, and collaborated with Elton John in Disney's *The Lion King*. His marvellous body of work stretches further, but you get the idea. One of the most celebrated lyricists in British popular culture, Tim Rice was knighted by Queen Elizabeth II for his services to music in 1994. He has a star on the Hollywood Walk of Fame, is an inductee into the Songwriter's Hall of Fame and a Disney Legend recipient. And among his many awards, Tim Rice won an Academy Award for Best Original Song, 'Can you feel the love tonight' (*The Lion King*).

But I asked him about celebrities and cricket. 'Well, it seems people involved in the theatre especially come to love the game of cricket,' he said. I remember meeting Trevor Howard in Cape Town in 1970. 'Principally,' he laughed, 'I'm here to enjoy good Stellenbosch reds and see the Test match, but I do have a commitment to my job. You see the film *Battle of Britain* (starring Howard, Sir Lawrence Olivier and company) is about to be showcased across the republic's cinemas. It opens in Cape Town and so does the Australia–South Africa first Test at Newlands. I always like to have a project in the very time and place a Test match is being played.'

That South African summer we had Norman Wisdom bowl to us in Durban and he got most of us cheaply in the nets, except for Bill Lawry who defended Wisdom's curly stuff (off a long, animated approach) as if his life depended on it.

'I toured Albania with Norman many years ago,' Tim smiled.

In 1972, Mick Jagger, who loves his cricket and especially fast bowlers, came to our team hotel in the Aldwych and had the odd half pint of Double Diamond with Dennis and the rest of us. I mentioned to Tim that I wished to get in touch with Mick and perhaps have him featured in this book.

'Well, I'm having Christmas lunch with him in a few weeks ...'

Cricket is as much in Tim Rice's blood as the theatre. Tim wrote a lively cricket column in the *Daily Telegraph* for years, delving into the historical and the quirky; areas of the game not usually crafted by the regular cricket writers on staff. Tim also started the Heartaches Cricket Club and the club has been going for more than 45 years.

Cricket, a musical for Queen Elizabeth's 60th birthday, was Andrew Lloyd Webber and Tim Rice's final collaboration. The work was commissioned by the Queen's youngest son, Prince Edward. Rice and Lloyd Webber created a brilliant 25-minute 'musicalette': the production entirely sung through with no spoken dialogue. The show debuted as planned on 18 June 1986 at Windsor Castle.

In 2002 Sir Tim Rice was president of the Marylebone Cricket Club (MCC). He comes to Australia regularly to watch the Tests and is highly sought as an after-dinner speaker. His love for theatre and cricket is insatiable. Perhaps that connection is apt for there was always high drama and theatre associated in the play of many of cricket's luminaries. In 1990 Tim, playing for Lord's Taverners, at Lord's, did what many could never do: capture the wicket of Colin Cowdrey.

> I must have been about 45, so still agile. There were a few first-class cricketers playing, such as Colin Cowdrey. My great achievement that day was getting Cowdrey out. It could have been a deliberate mistake by him, but I like to think he was baffled. The ball took the edge of his bat and was brilliantly caught by Willie Rushton. Colin said later: 'I think that was the message that I really should give up.'

Cowdrey: caught Rushton bowled Rice! I did happen to mention in our interview that Cowdrey was my very first Test wicket, at The Oval some 22 years earlier.

There are many famous quotations attributed to wordsmith Tim Rice. Here is one: 'I think failure is the best thing for some people. It tells you whether you're in the right job or the wrong one.' Tim Rice's articulate deliveries have been read or heard in a variety of forms over many seasons. When he bowls up those lyrical gems we field them and hang on to them for cherished moments, like the man at cover taking the ball low down and hanging on for dear life: a moment to savour.

No doubt there's been myriad Irishmen among the madding crowd who warm to Tim's fabulous lyrics. Some time back there came the lovely line by John Arlott, concerning Nottinghamshire's South African-born champion Clive Rice and the Irishman at cover. Arlott was patient. He waited for the right time. Finally a ball from Rice found its way to the Irishman at cover and Arlott came forth with this splendid poetic line: droll yet full of joy in his heavy Somerset accent: 'Rice bowls ... and Paddy fields.'

Chapter 35

Breaking the rhythm

The key to spin bowling success is how the ball arrives to the batsman. If the ball leaves the bowler's hand hard-spun and dipping, the area of danger for the spinner is enormous. However, even the hardest-spun, dipping delivery will not bring consistent results if every ball arrives at the same speed. If every ball is arriving on much the same trajectory at the same speed every single delivery will land in the same tiny area. A good batsman would soon get into his rhythm. 'Oh, here comes another one, landing in the same spot. Where will I smash it this time?' The batsman's dominance of the bowler will continue until the bowler changes tack.

What needs to change is his pace. A spinner can only hope to break the rhythm of the batsman by this sort of sequence: stock ball, stock ball, one slower, stock ball, stock ball, one slightly quicker. But how does a spinner achieve changing his pace in a subtle manner?

When I first attempted to change my pace, I found I couldn't do so without slowing my bowling arm so it was demonstrably slower than with my stock ball. As a teenager I watched Lance Gibbs often bowl his slower one by delivering the ball from a metre or so behind where he normally released the ball. A slower bowling arm was a dead giveaway to any batsman worth his salt, and the Gibbs method was a challenge to land in a good area because the ball had to travel another metre to reach the landing spot. The slightly faster ball was also easily read because I merely quickened the speed of my bowling arm. Most top-class batsmen will read the direction of spin, however, you don't want them to detect changes of pace. So the changes have to be very subtle; almost to the extent that watching from the fence every ball looks exactly the same in terms of trajectory and speed.

The slow-medium-paced off-cutter merchant of the 1890s, George Giffen, operated in his days of splendour by bringing many a 'caught and bowled' victim with his deceptive changes of pace. Australia's Steve O'Keeffe reminds me of a much slower version of Derek Underwood. Deadly could shore up an end on the flattest of wickets with variations usually so subtle he had talented Test batsman floundering to survive, let alone score freely. In February 2017, on the treacherous Pune first Test turner, O'Keeffe operated with unerring accuracy against the Indian right-handers who were forced to play every ball. Some of O'Keeffe's deliveries turned a little; some turned big and some scuttled straight on like an Exocet missile skimming just above the waves to find its inevitable target.

***

When I first came to South Australia in 1967 medium-fast merchant Neil Hawke counselled me on the nature of the Adelaide Oval wicket. 'It's dead as a dodo; flat as anything you'll ever encounter in this game at first-class level; no spin, no bounce, nothing. You'll have to find something in your repertoire to make a difference.'

Hawkeye was wrong. After bowling on the granite-hard tracks in Perth grade cricket, where you had to spin the cover off the ball to get it to move from the straight and narrow, Adelaide Oval was a dream. The ball spun appreciably and there was ample bounce. As the game wore on there was greater spin and the bounce became increasingly more variable. Yet I knew Hawkeye was right about one thing: I needed subtle changes of pace and I had to find a way, fast. My early efforts to find subtle change of pace in my bowling were abject failures. To sharpen my fielding reflexes so I could fulfil my plan to become a good gully fieldsman, I had a habit of throwing a golf ball at a wall and catching the rebound. It was a terrific exercise because if you threw the ball at a casual pace it came back smartly; if you threw it fast it returned at breakneck speed. It was either a case of catching the golf ball or wearing it.

Then one day I couldn't find a golf ball, so I picked up a cricket ball and began bowling at the wall from a standing start. I stood about 10 metres from the wall but the standing start was no good, I needed movement, so I banged in a stump, marked out my normal approach and bowled a stock ball. Interestingly I found that after a few balls I could feel how my stock ball should feel out of the hand. After an over, I noticed that the stock ball was generally hitting the same brick on the wall, so I grabbed a lump of chalk and marked the brick with an X.

'What then would a subtle slower ball feel like?' I pondered. It was at that very moment, my light bulb moment, it dawned on me. If I marked the brick above the stock ball brick with an X and the brick below the stock ball brick with an X then bowled at each target brick I might be able to change my pace in a subtle way without having to slow or quicken my bowling arm. I bowled four stock balls and they all hit the middle brick X, as planned. Then I tried the brick above, my slower one. It hit the brick smack in the middle. In reality I had released the ball slightly earlier than I would for my stock ball. This happened naturally, without my having to think about releasing the ball a little earlier. My slightly quicker ball also worked a treat. I had found a way.

By training in this way I got the feel of each of those deliveries: the stock ball, the slower one, the faster one. I spent many hours at the nets working on a change of pace. After lots of training, my subtle changes of pace created greater belief in me. Yes, I had found a way to change the pace. Now I needed to be able to do so with the same accuracy and confidence I had with my stock ball.

At Swansea in 1968, Australia was playing Glamorgan and the little left-hander Alan Jones had worked his way to 99. Neil Hawke was at mid-on. I said to Hawkeye: 'Mate, move back thirty yards. He's going to try to hit me over the top.' Unconvinced Hawkeye sauntered back towards the mid-on rope. In my mind's eye I could see the 'top brick X' as I released the ball. The feel was perfect. Jones had a slog, wasn't to the pitch and Hawke gobbled the skied catch about 15 yards inside the mid-on boundary.

Then in my first Test at The Oval in the August of that year I bowled a great deal to Basil D'Oliveira, who scored a fabulous 158, yet I had him missed three times – all with my slower ball – before finally getting him with a misjudged sweep off my stock off-break. Earlier on the first day I had held one back to Ted Dexter, who duly obliged by hitting me a return catch, which I floored. It wasn't a wicket, but definitely a moral victory for he didn't read the slower one. I was convinced by then that my brick wall strategy was working for me.

A season later, in a Test against the West Indies at the Gabba, I bowled a ball to Rohan Kanhai who hit the ball with the spin, one bounce over mid-on to take his score to 96. I sensed that he was going again, so I said to captain Bill Lawry: 'Phantom put CHO (Johnny Gleeson) back, I reckon Rohan's going to try that again.'

'You're mad ... he's on 96. He won't do anything silly.'

'Phantom, his name is Rohan Kanhai, not Bill Lawry.'

Bill refused to move Gleeson back, but I quietly urged CHO to do so and he did, getting back about 30 paces. The very next ball – the top brick X slower ball – lured Kanhai into having a go and it landed safely in the hands of Gleeson.

Years later I was coaching in New Zealand with Dennis Lillee in Otago. Lillee was working with the emerging speedsters and I looked after 60 spinners. On the edge of the field was a long and impressive-looking brick wall. Perfect. I called the youngsters together and explained to them the virtues of change of pace, a vital part of their learning about becoming a good spinner. In addition I told them my story; how I found a way to change my pace in a subtle manner. I banged in 20 stumps, all about five paces apart. There were three bowlers at each stump. Each bowler marked out his normal run from the stump and marked the turf. We had a trial run whereby each bowler got the feel of his stock ball and the brick was marked; same with the other balls, slower and faster.

As the first bowler released the ball, he would fetch the rebound and move to the back of the line. Every couple of seconds 20 balls would hit the brick wall and those hits were resounding over a fair distance along the back of this impressive building. All went well until a small, bearded chap rushed across the turf yelling, 'Stop, stop this carnage.' My protest at this rude intrusion fell on deaf ears.

BREAKING THE RHYTHM

'I am the curator of the Dunedin Art Gallery ...' Picture the scene: the incessant noise of 20 balls banging on the outside wall of the gallery; and I could see famous works of art crashing to the floor.

Before he went to India in 2001, champion Australian opener Matthew Hayden used to struggle against quality spin bowling. He liked to hit boundaries, as most fast bowlers who bowled to him would attest. However, a good spinner could tie him down and he wasn't the type of player to work singles and twos to break a bowler's rhythm. Hayden liked to dominate and hit the ball powerfully. He devised a method for the Indian tour to slog-sweep the spinners. He did so successfully and belted all and sundry, even Harbhajan Singh, who had long been a menacing threat against the Australian batsmen. Why did Hayden succeed playing this way? Well, he had a long reach, he wielded a big bat and even a top-edge was likely to cruise over the boundary. I believe he mostly succeeded because the spin bowlers didn't change their pace in a subtle enough manner: too much difference between the stock ball and the pace of the slower one, the stock ball and the faster one.

In 1969 the brilliant Indian off-spinner Erapally Prasanna was able to pin our batsmen to the crease, even the likes of that great player of spin bowling, Ian Chappell. Prasanna got the ball above the eye line, hard spun and dipping wickedly, but his change of pace was the greatest of his assets for he seemed during one delivery to have the ball on a string and haul it back his way when the batsman advanced. Next ball would be a little flatter and quicker and the batsman would stumble forward slamming down quickly lest it crash into the stumps. He continually changed his pace and his pattern of those changes: watching him weave his magic was compelling viewing.

Breaking the rhythm of the batsman is paramount. Today we hear from the TV commentators all about the need to change pace in the limited overs form of the game, yet rarely do they mention change of pace to defeat the best of batsmen in Test cricket. Most top batsmen seek to break the rhythm of the spinner by rotating the strike, working through gaps and keeping the scoreboard ticking over, for they know a frustrated spinner, no matter how good, will, under such circumstance, dish up more easy pickings.

The great leg-spinner of the Bradman era, Bill O'Reilly, stands shoulder-to-shoulder with Shane Warne and Clarrie Grimmett among the three best spin bowlers Australia has produced. Don Bradman regarded O'Reilly as the best of all. A splendid wordsmith, to my mind the best of all former Test players who turned their hand to writing after they hung up their boots. For years O'Reilly wrote an informative and entertaining regular summer column for the *Sydney Morning Herald*. One of O'Reilly's last pieces of writing was the foreword he wrote for *Scarlet*, my biography of Clarrie Grimmett.

The Tiger wrote, in part:

> He (Clarrie) sized up a batsman in a few deliveries and concentrated on bowling straight at the stumps and landing the ball in the chosen awkward spot, which demanded expert use of batting feet. He never resorted to 'loop', as onlookers call it, but he was an expert in the covert change of pace, which was the very backbone of his undisputed claim to be the greatest of his tribe.

Emerging spinners need to master three things – hard-spun, dipping deliveries backed by subtle changes of pace. If you can do these things consistently you are well on the way.

Chapter 36

Gubby Allen: the England bowler who defied Jardine

One day at golf, under the warmth of God's sunshine, former Test all-rounder and leading MCC administrator Gubby Allen was stung by the venom of Douglas Bader's words.

Like some wounded German fighter bomber the *Battle of Britain* hero's seven iron had limped towards a tree at the edge of the fairway and disappeared into the rough. Bader thumped along the tall grass on his tin legs before he fell in a tangled heap on the ground. While he struggled in vain to right himself, there was no cry of alarm from the determined RAF *Spitfire* legend.

Eventually Allen began a search for his friend. He found him lying on his back, his tin legs crossed. When Bader's artificial legs become entangled in that way it was impossible for him to get himself back to an upright position. Bader needed help right then and there lest he spend the rest of the day lying helplessly on his back in the tall grass. Allen extended his hand and Bader waved his seven iron threateningly about his head and bellowed, 'Fuck off, Allen!' Silence. Neither of the two friends would budge. But Bader's predicament was all too clear to them both. He would have to concede and ask Allen's assistance. 'Okay, okay. I'll accept your help. Give me a hand?' 'I'll help you, Douglas, on one condition and one only.' Neither wanted to give ground, but Bader saw the futility in being stubborn and eventually he muttered something to the effect that he was sorry and Allen helped him up. The sporting gods of the Berkshire Golf Club sighed relief.

George Oswald Browning 'Gubby' Allen was born on 31 July 1902 in Bellevue Hill, Sydney, the second of three children to lawyer Walter Allen and his wife, Marguerite (nee Lamb), the daughter of Queensland's Minister of Lands. In 1909 when he was six years old, the Allen family moved back to England where his parents believed Gubby would get a far better education than he would in Australia in the years leading up to WWI.

After playing cricket for Eton College, Allen played for Cambridge University and Middlesex as a hard-hitting lower-order batsman and fast bowler. He played 25 Tests for England – 'one of us against us' – leading the side on 11 occasions. In all he hit 750 Test runs at 24.19 with a high of 122 and took 81 wickets at 29.37.

He debuted for Middlesex in 1921, but as was the case with many an amateur player there were infrequent matches under his belt before fortune fell upon him with a better job to allow more county cricket and he made his Test debut against Bill Woodfull's 1930 Australian side at Lord's in 1930. When Australia batted, a young man named Don Bradman hit a almost flawless 254 in the team total of 729. Bradman always described that innings as the best he ever played. 'Even the ball in which I was dismissed was hit sweetly, a couple of inches off the ground, and the England skipper Percy Chapman dived to catch the ball inches from the turf,' Bradman told me when I interviewed him in Adelaide in 1974. Gubby Allen didn't fare so well. With the bat he scored 3 and 57 and his only turn at the crease with the ball he bowled 34 overs for a fruitless none for 115.

Gubby forged a good relationship with Bradman. It probably grew from Allen's stance on Bodyline. Like his friend Douglas Bader, Allen was stubborn to a tee and he refused to use Douglas Jardine's intimidatory tactics of bowling bouncers almost every ball to all opposing batsmen to a packed leg-side field. The summer of 1932–33 will go down in cricket history as a tour of infamy.

The Bodyline tactic was largely designed by the England captain Douglas Jardine, who was hell-bent upon curbing the prolific scoring of Bradman. Allen was one of four fast bowlers chosen for the tour, but he did not go along with Jardine's instructions to 'intimidate and hate' their Australian opponents. In the first tour match Allen unsettled and dismissed Bradman with his pace. In later years Jack Hobbs, who covered the tour as a newspaper correspondent, suggested that Bradman was intimidated by Allen. The England all-rounder, who defied Jardine, later wrote to his father penning the extraordinary claim that 'Bradman was a terrible little coward of fast bowling'. It seems that Bradman was never aware of what Allen wrote in his letter because the pair became friends. Both men became stockbrokers: Allen from 1933 on his return from Australia, and Bradman worked first for Harry Hodgetts when lured from Sydney to Adelaide in 1935, and then set up his own business when Hodgetts fell on his sword and went to jail for fraud.

In the Bodyline series Allen took 21 wickets at an average of 28.28. In all first-class games in Australia that summer Allen scored 397 runs at 24.81 and took 39 wickets at 23.05. Throughout the series Allen refused to bowl Bodyline and his attitude, while winning favour with the Australian public, incensed Jardine. The England captain twice tried to force the issue, but Allen flatly refused. 'Douglas, that is not the way I want to play cricket. If you are not happy with my stance then you can easily drop me from the team.' On the second occasion Jardine tried to win Allen over, he told him that his fellow fast bowlers, Harold Larwood and Bill Voce, were keen that he join them in the Bodyline tactic. Messrs Larwood and Voce found professional cricket to be a way out of the backbreaking toil as miners.

Allen, who was soon to pursue a career on the London Stock Exchange, wrote home: 'Well I burst and said a good deal about swollen-headed, gutless, uneducated miners.' When Allen threatened not to play and to go home and to relate the events of the tour to the press, Jardine dropped the matter like a hot cake. Upon his return to England Allen continued to oppose the Bodyline tactic and he made his opinion known to senior figures in the Marylebone Cricket Club (MCC), including Sir Pelham Warner. He led a debate among county representatives which resulted in legislation to ban the Bodyline tactic after the 1934 summer.

As a stockbroker Allen's cricket availability with Middlesex and England was limited, yet he was appointed captain of the England team which toured Australia in 1936–37. Australian won a fabulous series 3–2, after trailing 2-nil. He continued to turn out irregularly for Middlesex until 1939 and served in military intelligence during WWII. Allen became a long-serving MCC administrator, was deeply involved in the Basil d'Oliveira affair and in 1971, thanks to the foresight of Allen and Bradman, then both key cricket administrators, the first One Day International was played between Australia and England in wake of the Test match being washed out. He served as MCC President in 1963 and was knighted in 1986. Sir George Oswald Browning 'Gubby' Allen died in his St John's Wood flat, no more than a Don Bradman drive from his beloved Lord's Cricket Ground.

Chapter 37

Erapalli Prasanna: spin wizard

Erapalli Prasanna was far and away the greatest off-spinner of my experience. And I've seen plenty of good ones along the way including Jim Laker, Graeme Swann, Muttiah Muralitheran, Lance Gibbs, Tim May, Bruce Yardley, John Bracewell, Harbijan Singh, Nathan Lyon and Ravi Ashwin among the best. Pras stands out for me as the greatest for he had the ball on a string. Cricket correspondent Uday Rajan described Prasanna's art beautifully when he wrote in June 2009: 'Pras was like a chess player in the guise of an off-spinner: his victims had often been out-thought before the ball had been delivered.'

Facing Pras was some experience. He came in at a leisurely gait and the ball seemed to be propelled with a sudden heave of the shoulder. Then came the buzzing, fluttering sound of the ball fizzing in the air. He was the master of flight, tough to play even on the flint-hard pitches of Australia. Batsmen were often mesmerised by his craft; you were lured to your doom by the tantalising flight path and the sweet humming of the ball as it came at you like a red sphere of bees. You'd play forward to Pras expecting to meet the ball nicely and smother any spin before it had a chance to make mischief off the inside (or outside) edge. But there was rarely a chance to get the ball on the half volley, for it was as if Pras, the puppetmaster, had the ball on a string, and was pulling it towards him at the other end, away from your desperate forward lunge.

Pras developed an 'away' ball, which sometimes seemed to bobble in the air as if the torment of the hard spun, dipping off-breaks were enough to have you squinting, scratching and scraping to survive another ball – let alone an over or two more in the middle.

Pras played the first few of his 49 Test matches in 1961–62, then he spun out of big cricket for five years, during which time he finished his undergraduate studies. In 1967, Pras returned and immediately became the favourite weapon of Indian captain The Nawab of Pataudi. Tiger Pataudi relied on him a great deal in Australia in the 1967–68 summer, and the brilliant offie never let his skipper down. He took something in the order of 25 wickets and impressed all and sundry, including such spin-bowling luminaries as Bill O'Reilly and Clarrie Grimmett, with his artistry.

When Bill Lawry's Australians toured India in 1969 it was Prasanna and his left-arm orthodox spin partner Bishen Bedi who worried the Australian batting most of all. Ian Chappell, who had a boom Indian summer with the bat, said later:

> I thought Pras was a genius. He had beautiful flight with his off-the-shoulder style action. So many times when the ball left his hand, it appeared to be an invitation to a juicy half volley, but it never kept the appointment. I used to wonder whether Pras had the ball on a string, which he tugged just as you were about to play the shot. He was equally adept at spinning a web of confusion on both the hard Australian pitches and on the more receptive pitches in India. Pras enjoyed bowling to batsmen who were prepared to go after him. In fact he would say: 'I like to think a spinner should bowl in such a way that he is inviting him to hit him into the outfield.' His theory put in another way might suggest that with a hard-spun, dipping flight path the ball would drop short of the batsman and thus strike the bat very high, near the splice.

Among Lawry's men in India, Chappell and Doug Walters played the spinners best. However, the two Australians differed in their opinions about just whom was the better bowler – Prasanna or Bedi. Chappell said there was no argument: 'Pras was easily the best spinner.' Walters believed it was Bedi. Interestingly Walters came forward with a crooked bat, so the more the off-spinner spun it the more likely it was for the ball to be met by the full face of his bat. Chappell always said Walters was the greatest player of off-spin bowling he ever saw.

In that 1969 series, Prasanna took 26 wickets and Bedi 25. It was very much a saga of the spinners for yours truly managed to take 28 wickets in a rubber which the Australians were lucky to win 3–1. It could easily have gone the other way.

Whenever an Australian team tours India today the spinners in the team should take time out to have a chat with Erapalli Prasanna. I know he was good for me in 1969. He spoke a little like Clarrie Grimmett in terms of flight – hard-spun stuff just above eye level – but he put the same idea in a different way.

One of my enduring memories is watching Prasanna duel with Chappell at Delhi. Pras would bring him forward one ball, perhaps two, both hard-spun whirling deliveries which, if Chappelli didn't cover the spin, the ball would whip the turf like a striking cobra; ever-present danger. Ball three might be a shade faster, but with that hard-spun whirling sound and dipping arc, but designed to trap the batsman on the crease. Such contests are the ecstasy of cricket.

How would Prasanna fare in today's international cricket? I believe Pras at his best would be a sensation. During an interview in India in recent times he said, 'I and Bishen (Bedi) would be a success today. We had flight, dipping flight and turn. And we studied batsmen.' Pras believed greatly in the psychology of cricket.

In 1970–71, India played a tour game in Jamaica. 'Lawrence Rowe was one of the players everyone was talking about,' said Pras. 'He got off to a good start and even though I was bowling well, he was playing me comfortably. As he played each ball, he whistled. I thought, What the hell, man? The ball was hanging in the air and dipping but he was smothering the spin quite comfortably. So I went to the umpire (Douglas Sang Hue) and said, "Look, Lawrence is whistling and it is distracting my fieldsmen."

Umpire Sang Hue asked Rowe to stop whistling and he replied, "Yeah, okay." The very next Prasanna delivery he was caught at forward short leg.

'Ah,' laughed Pras, 'Lawrence was distracted momentarily ... his mind was on the whistling.'

Erapalli Prasanna was the best offie of them all. He seemed to embrace flight of a cricket ball like some sort of aeronautical genius.

Chapter 38

Catalyst for change

Minutes after Ian and Greg Chappell chased down the runs for SA to beat NSW at the SCG to win the coveted Sheffield Shield, I bumped into Richie Benaud at the dressing-room door.

'Ah, Rowdy,' he said with a smile, 'India awaits. You'll find it a very interesting experience.'

This was February 1969 and the tour did not get underway until after the Australian winter. I decided to get myself fit and took on a job lugging wheat-bag-sized bags of flour about in an Adelaide factory all day, five days a week for about two months, then I took the train to Perth to see my parents. A few weeks later I was on the Indian Pacific returning to Adelaide before embarking on the oddest cricket tour of them all.

The players congregated in Sydney. Our manager, Fred Bennett, drilled us about the excitement of the Indian crowds and their unbridled joy of cricket. The plan was: two weeks in Ceylon (now Sri Lanka) where we'd play one unofficial Test; then nearly four months in India where five Tests were scheduled and, finally, on to South Africa and a further four Tests.

What Bennett failed to tell us was the then Australian Board of Control for International Cricket (subsequently renamed the Australian Cricket Board, mainly at the insistence of Sir Donald Bradman; now Cricket Australia) booked us into the shabbiest, cheapest hovels of hotels in India. Little wonder Bradman wanted the word 'control' cut from the Board's official title, for this tour of Ceylon, India and South Africa proved the catalyst for World Series Cricket.

Ceylon was a pleasant enough place and the people were friendly and always smiling. They had some pretty good cricketers but the nation was years away from being admitted into the international Test cricket family. One player in particular caught my attention. I was on a visit to the Nondescripts Cricket Club (NCC) in Colombo where Pat McCarthy was a legend. There on the wall behind the bar of the clubhouse was a photograph of McCarthy, his cap at a tilt and wearing a smile as big as the historic once-grand colonial edifice down the road known as the Galle Face Hotel, our digs in the city that tour. By 1969, when the Australian Cricket Team stayed there, the place was pretty much a hovel; cockroaches and rats were often observed in the players' rooms. The actual building still retained a brilliant colonial dignity ... from the outside. At least the renowned Galle Face Hotel omelettes were fabulous then, as they are today.

Well before Bill Lawry's Australian Cricket Team of 1969 arrived, celebrity guests included an array of people including Mahatma Gandhi, Yuri Gagarin, the first man in space, John D. Rockefeller, Prince Phillip, the Duke of Edinburgh, MI6 agent F.W. Winterbottom, Prince Hirohito of Japan, Roger Moore, Carrie Fisher, Richard Nixon, Lord Louis Mountbatten, 1st Earl Mountbatten of Burma, Noel Coward and Josip Broz Tito, Marshall of Yugoslavia. In January 2018 His Royal Highness Prince Edward and the Countess of Wessex spent a day or so at the Galle Face Hotel during their five-day visit to Sri Lanka. Pity we didn't see the hotel in its glory back in 1969.

But I digress: my interest in Pat McCarthy was due to his playing for the Mount Lawley Cricket Club after emigrating from Ceylon to Australia in 1948. Mount Lawley was the club I played for from 1955–1967 before moving to Adelaide. McCarthy scored two double centuries, 10 centuries, and more than 50 half centuries for the Colombo-based NCC. Then in the 1950–51 summer he scored 870 runs for Mount Lawley, a long-held record for Perth grade cricket.

Towards the end of that record-breaking grade summer, McCarthy made his first-class debut for WA, hitting a hurricane 88 against SA in his second match when he added 90 in 80 minutes with Wally Langdon. My family did not move to Perth from Sydney until 1955. A year earlier I had stood in the sun at the SCG with my Chatswood Public schoolmates awaiting the arrival of Queen Elizabeth II and the Duke of Edinburgh. During that first Royal visit, on 6 February 1954, the Duke of Edinburgh was at the SCG to watch WA play NSW and Pat McCarthy, along with John Rutherford and Arnold Byfield, added 61 runs in 45 minutes. McCarthy, a swarthy, laidback sort of batsman, smashed the ball with ferocious force majestic in its artistry. The Duke was delighted to witness McCarthy's brilliant 98. One Sydney-based cricket writer described his innings as being of 'almost prehistoric majesty and virility'. This cricketing life turns up lots of coincidences and links: well, it does for me.

***

The unofficial Test in Kandy ended in a tame draw and it was off to India. I found myself a starter of the first Test in Bombay (now Mumbai) and we had India on the ropes at 8/125 in their second innings, chasing plenty, when all hell broke loose. (For the story of the riot that day, read Chapter 15.)

My contribution to the easy win wasn't great (30 overs 0/43 in the first dig and 2/22 in the second), however, it didn't take too long before I realised that length was the key to spin bowling in India. I watched Erapalli Prasanna, the great Indian offie, operating against the better players of spin in the Australian team: Ian Chappell and Doug Walters. Prasanna was constantly on the attack. He got the ball to dip more than me, although I had the ball curving late. We were completely different in style and method, but it worked for us both on that tour.

Change of pace was also vital and Pras did that better than any spinners in my experience. Batsmen brought up on wickets in the Subcontinent tend to look to hit the spinner square of the wicket. Recent tours of India and Sri Lanka by Australian teams have seen this method of batting all too often despite the likes of Nathan Lyon starting to get the idea about length on these slow, yet very receptive, spinning wickets.

A couple of years back at the National Cricket Centre in Brisbane there was much ado about how to bowl on the spin-friendly Indian tracks. There were lots of graphs produced on where the runs were scored by Indian batsmen over a few tours. Prasanna always advocated that length was the key on any wicket. Logically there is a different length on a flint-hard wicket, such as we get in Australia, and a slow turner in England or New Zealand, and a treacherous spinning deck on the Subcontinent. Any spinner in India must adapt and adapt swiftly to the type of wicket he confronts. Because of the extra bounce on Australian tracks the spinner's length can afford to be shorter than on a slower deck. The spinners who do not adapt to the Indian tracks probably bowl the same sort of length they are accustomed to bowling in Australia. They find, to their annoyance, that they are continually being hit square of the wicket, either just in front of point to the left of cover on the off side, and in front of square leg to the right of mid-wicket on the leg side. In all cases the spinner being worked square in this manner is due to one vital factor: poor length.

After the first Test we travelled to Jaipur, the capital of Rajasthan, a peaceful little town that boasted the cricketing might of Central Zone. The instant I alighted from the bus a thin little man rushed to my side. 'Oh, Mr Mallett, I am begging you, please may I carry your bag?' He didn't introduce himself, but I was glad of his help for we all had at least one suitcase and one cricket bag. In 1969 there were no wheels on cases or cricket cases to ease the burden: you simply gathered yourself for the lift and carried on. When I was brought on to bowl, the umpire looked familiar. Why, umpire S. Roy was the little bloke who kindly offered to carry my bags.

Vijay Pimrikar must have been the unluckiest batsman to ever walk to the crease. My off break pitched middle and leg and the manner in which the ball was turning on that dry, dusty track it might well have missed a second set of stumps had not Pimprikar got his left pad in the road.

The Australian all-rounder Cecil Pepper, turned umpire, encouraged me to appeal when we toured England in 1968. 'Don't leave them wondering. Always ask the question.' My appeal for LBW was upheld in the most emphatic way by this umpire-cum-baggage-man. Next fellow, Rajeev Sharma, wasn't keen to get his pad anywhere near the ball. I tried to spin an off break, but the ball upon pitching carried on straight. Sharma played for spin and the ball beat his outside edge by the proverbial mile and hit the top of his off stump. At over's end, Doug Walters, ever on the lookout for the unusual and bizarre on the cricket field, strolled over to umpire Roy.

'A couple of useful deliveries Mr Umpire?'

'Oh, yes, Mr Walters ... that Mallett ... welly good bowler. The first ball to Pimprikar was a top spinner and the next ball, to Sharma, was a perfectly pitched leg-break.'

I finished with 7/38 that dig and 10/80 for the match. We should have employed umpire Roy to officiate at all our matches, including the Tests.

We won the series in India 3/1. We had riots in Bombay (Mumbai) and Kanpur. Stones were cast during riots in Bombay and in the team bus travelling from the ground to the airport in Calcutta and we stayed at some of the most ramshackle dumps of hotels imaginable: you know the drill, stagnant water, running rats and wall-to-wall cockroaches. The food was disgusting and the hygiene non-existent. It could (and should) have been so much better if the cricket Board back home had booked us into decent hotels, of which there were many. The Board had shown that the players' welfare wasn't a priority.

There were reports out of Australia from prominent past players calling for the tour to be cancelled in the wake of news reports filtering back to Australia about our bus being stoned. Former champion all-rounder Alan Davidson, who knew all about the health issues of touring India, having toured there in 1959–60, said: 'No sporting side should be subjected to the humiliations our team have encountered in India. Our players are subject to enough risk already to their health in a place like India without adding physical dangers.' Ex Test opening batsman Jim Burke said: 'The stoning is just about the end. Stones this time, but is it going to be knives next?' Concern for the players' welfare, however, did not run as far as officials of the cricket Board back home. We later learnt that each player was insured for the princely sum of $400.

To me the cricket itself was fabulous. I loved the matches, the pitches, Dougie Walters loved the umpires, and the amazing enthusiasm of the cricket fans. And there were some amusing moments. For my 6/64 in the third Test against India at New Delhi I was presented with a brand-new, tailored suit. Down the track I had it dry cleaned, but in reality I think the cleaning company subcontracted the job to a lesser laundry firm and it was returned with the buttons broken, as if they had been subjected to pressure. In India, if your laundry was near the Ganges River, or any river for that matter, clothes were cleaned by thrashing them against stones on the edge of the water. Walters sent in his long-sleeved Test pullover and it came back a number of sizes too small, a perfect fit for Paddington Bear.

Lawry's team flew from Bombay to Nairobi on New Year's Eve, 1969. There we stayed for two or three days. The food was terrific but we hardly touched it for our stomachs had shrunken. In South Africa for four Tests we discovered a far superior standard of accommodation. However, because we were used to sleeping on thin horse-hair mattresses over a bed of sawn planks in India, the beds in the republic were too soft, so we bunked down on the floor. Many of the players were malnourished. One, Graham McKenzie, contracted a form of hepatitis and that, plus other ongoing health issues among the team, accounted to a degree for our performance on the field. We lost the four Test series 4–nil. Out batting and fielding was abysmal, the umpiring was awful, but we deserved to lose so heavily because the home side was easily the best team.

McKenzie returned 1/300, his only wicket being that of Springbok captain Ali Bacher pulling him to the boundary and in so doing treading on his stumps. Ian Chappell, who averaged 324 runs at 46.28, Keith Stackpole (368 at 46) and Doug Walters (286 at 40.85) in India all struggled against South Africa. Chappell scored 92 runs at 11.50; Walters 258 runs at 32.25 and Stackpole 187 runs at 23.37 in the four Test series.

Near the end of the tour the South Africans wanted to host a fifth Test at the Wanderers Ground in Johannesburg. Back home our Board agreed to a fifth Test and offered to pay each Australian player $300 to play. The Test never took place (read Chapter 23 for the full story). Bill Lawry took it upon himself to write to the Board about the players' concerns over accommodation in India, the itinerary and the players' welfare. Ian Chappell and Ian Redpath in particular, pleaded with Lawry to have all of the tour party sign the letter of protest Lawry sent to the Board, but the Phantom was adamant. He felt duty bound for himself as captain to take the responsibility to voice the players' concerns. That was the beginning of the end for Lawry as captain and player.

CATALYST FOR CHANGE

The seven-month tour of Ceylon, India and South Africa, for which each player received something like $2700, plus airfares, accommodation, meals and laundry, was a national disgrace. The disgrace was largely unknown until stories began to emerge when the players returned to Australia, but that tour undoubtedly was the catalyst for change Down Under. It proved the perfect pathway for Kerry Packer and his revolutionary World Series Cricket.

Chapter 39

Clarrie Grimmett

In 248 first-class matches Clarrie Grimmett took bags of five wickets or more in a single innings 127 times. Don Bradman hit 117 centuries in 234 matches. If you equate a five-wicket haul with a century, Grimmett's bowling record is better than Bradman's batting record.

Born in New Zealand, Grimmett's burning ambition was to play Test cricket. In 1914 he set sail for Sydney; then to Melbourne, finally Adelaide, the 'haven for unwanted bowlers ...' Vic Richardson wanted Grimmett in his team. An immediate success for SA, Grimmett made his Test debut in the final Ashes contest of the 1924–25 summer at the SCG taking 11/82. Some debut.

From 1924–1941 Grimmett wheeled down 28,467 balls for South Australia and he still heads the all-time wicket tally in the Sheffield Shield with 513 wickets at 25.29. In 37 Tests he took 216 wickets at 24.21 and in first-class cricket he bagged 1424 wickets at 22.58 with a career best single innings effort of 10/37 against Yorkshire in 1930.

He always wore a scarlet woollen vest under his cricket shirt and while he was often called 'Grum' and 'the old fox', his best-known nickname was 'Scarlet'.

Grimmett dismissed Bradman 10 times in his career, including the Grimmett–Richardson Testimonial match at Adelaide Oval in November 1937. Late on the Friday Vic Richardson said: 'Scarlet, we need a wicket badly, but we also want Bradman to stay for the bumper crowd tomorrow.' Bradman had inferred that Grimmett had lost his ability to turn his leg-break. Just before stumps, Grimmett spun a leg-break prodigiously to defeat the master: Bradman bowled Grimmett 17.

Clarrie gave a triumphant jig and Richardson yelled: 'Scarlet, you bloody fool. You've just cost us a thousand quid!' But for Clarrie his craft with the ball was priceless: it was his breath of life. Grimmett stands alongside Bill O'Reilly and Shane Warne as the greatest of their tribe.

Chapter 40

Greg Chappell made batting look all so easy

Greg Chappell made batting look the easiest thing in the world. You know class when you pick up a book and start to read. The words flow effortlessly and you are lulled into the false mindset that it was all too easy for this writer. Truth is, the easiest passages to read are the hardest ones to write. Similarly with Chappell the runs flowed so effortlessly off his bat that you were lulled into a false sense: surely no one could make the likes of Andy Roberts, Joel Garner, Malcolm Marshall and company look lesser lights in the greater scheme of things? 'GC', as he was known, could.

His early cricket and backyard tussles with brothers Ian and Trevor are the stuff of legend. The boys are from good sporting stock. Their father Martin was a top flight baseballer and good grade cricketer and their mother, Jeanne, was the daughter of Victor Richardson, arguably Australia's greatest all-round sportsman: Test cricketer, baseballer and Australian Rules footballer. Richardson kept pretty much in the background with the boys' sporting progress. He left the hands-on stuff to Martin and friend Lyn Fuller, who taught the Chappell boys the rudiments of good technique. But Vic was rarely at the ground when the boys played. He kept his distance. Ian never seemed to know when Vic was there, but Greg knew. He could focus on his game like no one else and he was always aware of his surroundings.

From very early on Greg could catch a hard cricket ball. His father Martin once told me how he trained Greg to catch. 'You see dads everywhere trying to help teach their kids to catch a football or a cricket ball, but the youngster never gets it; his eyes are on dad, not the ball. Here's how I taught Greg,' Martin smiled.

One day he took Greg to a side wall of the family home. He held a cricket ball in his hand and underarmed the ball to the wall. Greg's eyes immediately shifted from looking at dad to eyeing the rebounding ball and within a few throws the two-year-old was catching the ball easily. In my experience this was one of the best coaching drills for youngsters: simple and easily achievable.

As kids growing up in the 1950s and 1960s we didn't (thank goodness) have a plethora of coaches fussing about the cricket nets analysing every stroke played, every ball bowled. The game was simple, just as it was meant to be, a game which has continued to evolve sensibly – that is before the change-for-change-sake boffins took up their stations. Think of players such as Keith Miller, the audacious all-rounder who never marked out his run, and Jeff Thomson, the man with the slingshot action, an action which might have been frowned upon by the change-for-change-sake boffins. Thankfully players of Greg Chappell's era were also spared this over-coaching nonsense we see today. Watching the ball closely seems to have been lost to many of today's batsmen. They take their eye off the ball when hooking or pulling the fast men – and how often do we witness a batsman being clobbered on the side of the helmet? GC's footwork was sublime. He's faced some of the fastest bowlers in history and has played them with a style and class befitting this great player.

GC hit a century on debut against England at Perth's WACA Ground in the summer of 1970–71. John Snow, the rangy England fast bowler, was a tough customer and GC had to call on all of his powers of concentration to get through the early overs. Snow wasn't blessed with hurricane speed like Jeff Thomson or Frank Tyson, but he had beautiful rhythm and could get the ball to rear at the batsman's ribcage. As the angular Ian Redpath swayed out of the way to frustrate Snow, Chappell gradually got on top of the England attack.

Ex England strokemaker Ted Dexter lauded GC's on-side play, especially the manner in which he got right up on his toes to flay the ball to anywhere he liked in the arc, from just in front of square leg to wide mid-on. His timing and placement that day, especially his hip shot, was spot on. Bradman later spoke publicly in an effort to justify the Chappell non-selection, by intimating that his batting would come on better playing a full season of Sheffield Shield than floundering against the spin of Erapally Prasanna and Bishen Bedi on the spin-friendly wickets in India, followed by having to change tack against South Africa's array of fast bowlers on green, bouncing wickets in the Republic. Perhaps Bradman was right for Jock Irvine, the WA batsman picked in place of GC, returned to Australia seemingly a broken batsman mentally, his bat metaphorically strapped to his pad. Jock played no more first-class cricket after the 1970–71 season in Australia.

Tellingly Sir Donald told me during a conversation at Adelaide Oval in 1974: 'We selectors copped a lot of flak over Greg Chappell missing out on the arduous tour of India and South Africa. It proved correct though for Greg has developed into a fine player. I don't think his development would have been as rapid had he toured India and spent his time carrying the drinks amid riots in Bombay and elsewhere.'

GC became a world-class player and must rank above most Australian batsmen to have played since the days of Bradman. Others, such as Ricky Ponting and Allan Border, have made more runs than GC but neither batsman is superior to him. There was more than a touch of the Grenadier guardsman about his bearing: tall, upright, head ever held high, a man who walked to the wicket or even into a room as if he was on a mission. When awaiting a bowler, Greg held his head perfectly still, eyes level. He lifted and lowered his bat in deliberate motion as the bowler moved in. Some thought they might sneak a yorker under the bat as it came down slowly, but this movement was always part of his rhythm. At the bowler's release GC was fiercely focused on the ball. He had the eye of an eagle, his footwork was sure and swift, and he always appeared to have oodles of time in which to play the fastest of bowlers.

A debut Test century, then 22 more before his 87th and final Test when he scored another century, 24 in all. Perhaps the most outstanding batting of his career was his 621 runs at an average of 69 in five 'Supertests' against the might of the West Indian pace attack on their home patch in 1979. Sadly,

GREG CHAPPELL MADE BATTING LOOK ALL SO EASY

World Series Cricket Supertests don't count for much in the record books; the statistics of those matches at home and abroad are not officially recorded.

I saw GC bat at close quarters and bowled to him in the nets. Because they were so highly competitive, bowling to Greg and Ian Chappell in the nets was an ideal way to judge just how well you were going. If I could bowl well to those guys the next day was a breeze in the psychological sense.

Jeff Thomson, arguably the fastest bowler to draw breath, has no hesitation in naming Greg Chappell as the greatest batsman of his era.

> I was batting with Greg in a Test match in New Zealand. Richard Hadlee was bowling and before he began a new over Greg came down the wicket. He had a gleam in his eye and he wore a wide grin. 'Hey, Thommo, watch this – I'm going to get stuck into the bowling now. Get a load of Richard Hadlee when I start to smash him. I'm gonna hit the ball high to leg. See those blokes,' he pointed to the man at deep backward square and the man deep in front, 'they'll probably run into each other.'
>
> I laughed. Thought is was just GC being a smart arse. But he was right. He belted the shit out of them. I saw Don Bradman, aged 70, bat at Doc Beard's backyard in Adelaide, but having played with and against Greg Chappell over many years and see him master good bowling under different conditions, I can't believe Don Bradman was twice as good as Greg Chappell.

Greg's ability to shut everything out of his mind and concentrate fully on the job at hand was, to me, legendary. He focused in a fierce manner. Meet GC today at a function and he eyeballs you; a raptor-like stare which demands your attention for however long the encounter lasts. As a captain he had, perhaps, one failing. So fierce was his concentration at second slip, I often got the feeling he forgot to make necessary bowling changes and left a bowler on too long. But that was minor fare in a career rich in runs, gloriously made in fabulous style, and superb fielding in the Mark Waugh ilk.

Gregory Stephen Chappell. Some player.

Chapter 41

The Big Cat

Meet Clive Lloyd – universally known as Big Cat. Tall (6 feet 5), stooped in the shoulders but immensely strong and lithe, Lloyd, at his best, was an athlete to behold. Off the field Clive is humble, his manner as gentle as a lamb, his voice soft and calm. But once the Big Cat bestrode the Test stage you'd swear he had changed personalities. He often wore a big white floppy hat instead of the regulation maroon Windies cap. There he stood, this giant of a man of the luxuriant moustache and dark horn-rimmed glasses. Ian Chappell liked to call Lloyd 'Groover' and when Big Cat got in the groove you knew you were in for it. At the wicket his three-pound cricket bat looked like a toothpick in his hands. He held the bat at the very top of the handle and through those horn-rimmed glasses his eyes focused with a penetrating intensity the very instant before he began to lay into any bowler who happened to be approaching.

In the 1975 World Cup at Lord's, Lloyd on a number of occasions smashed all-rounder Gary Gilmour straight back down, twice almost decapitating the Australian by the fierceness of his drives and prompting a newsman to asked Gilmour, 'How do you bowl to Clive Lloyd?' In the flashest of flashes, Gilmour said deadpan, 'With a crash helmet on!'

On 21 June 1975, the day of the historic first cricket World Cup final, Lloyd belted 12 fours and two sixes in an 85-ball 102, which set the West Indies up for a 17-run victory. Gilmour was the best of the Australian bowlers with

5/48 off 12 overs, but the Windies' brilliant fieldsman Viv Richards ran out three Aussie batsmen with direct hits. As Doug Walters quipped: 'There are no live rabbits in Antigua (Viv's home town).'

Lloyd's batting was fabulous, as his tally of 7515 Test runs with 19 centuries (242* v India in 1974 his best) at an average of 46.67 demonstrates. But his greatness as a batsman and as a superb fieldsman, either at cover early on or at first slip once the years began to slip by, was enhanced to legendary status by his captaincy. Clive Lloyd first led West Indies against India in Bangalore in 1974. His first stint as leader coincided with the Test debuts of Gordon Greenidge and Viv Richards. Greenidge had a great double (93 and 107), but Richards failed twice (4 and 3), before showing his mettle in the second Test at Feroz Shah Kotla, scoring a brilliant 192. Beating India 3-2 in his first series as Test captain was followed by two drawn Tests against Pakistan, then the famous World Cup title before Lloyd's West Indians toured Australia. The Australians were still smarting from their World Cup final loss and were determined to turn the tables on the tourists.

No doubt the wickets in England in 1975 were slowed to negate the pace and fire of Dennis Lillee and Jeff Thomson after they tore England apart in the 1974-75 Ashes summer. The Australian public loved the Windies, how they attacked at every opportunity. There would be colour and excitement in this series, no doubt. And the very first ball of the first Test at the Gabba saw Dennis Lillee's ball strike Greenidge on the front pad. Greenidge played no shot, there was a raucous appeal from the Australians and he was adjudged LBW. Next there was a flurry of expansive strokes and wickets tumbled at regular intervals. By lunch the West Indies had amassed 125 for the loss of six wickets: a morning of the bang, whack, wallop, ouch variety. The Windies batsmen lashed out with abandon, smashing a few fours, a six here and there, then out, usually hooking high in the air to a man on the fence or chasing a wide ball and snicking to slip. Eventually Lloyd's men were all out for 214. Lillee took 3/84 off just 11 overs; Thomson 1/69 off 10 and I chimed in with 1/1 off five balls. Australia won the match easily, with Greg Chappell, in his first Test as Australian captain, getting a hundred in each innings.

Next came the Perth second Test match. Ian Chappell hit a glorious 156 driving, hooking and cutting the Windies pace bowlers until the innings was over and in skipped the diminutive left-hander Roy Fredericks, who struck an amazing, whirlwind 169, smashing everyone in the Australian attack. The faster Lillee and Thomson came at Freddo, the harder he hit the ball. The little bloke batted with no fear. If it was short and wide he flung the bat at the ball. The ball either careered over the slips for four or found a gap all the way along the ground for a boundary. His first ball from Lillee set the pattern of the afternoon. A short, rising ball was hooked for six over fine leg. That was just the start of the carnage. That day in December 1975, the sky was blue and the sun shone over Perth but the fours rained in a torrent, telling all and sundry that this was an innings for the ages: a knock that would have delighted the likes of Trumper, Bradman, Harvey and Gilchrist. Freddo lit up the firmament in a star-studded display and in just 145 balls he had scorched to 169 and then, as suddenly as he took the game and everyone by storm, Fredericks was out. As he wandered back to the crease, all the Aussies stood about scratching their heads in disbelief: 'What just happened here?'

When something astonishing happens on the cricket field, and you've seen it all unfold before your very eyes, it is hard to comprehend. You need time to think. In my mind's eye I can see him now. There is Lillee hurling down his thunderbolts and Thomson bowling like the wind and Freddo cutting and pulling the two ferocious speedsters like a man possessed. There was many a time when Freddo cut at lifting deliveries and at the precise instant he struck the ball both of his feet were well clear of the ground. Perhaps a like player to Roy Fredericks today is David Warner, but Freddo didn't possess the sort of tree trunk of a bat Warner wields.

Ian Chappell's 156 was a fabulous knock, for the West Indies had some pretty good tearaway fast bowlers themselves. Bowlers of the calibre of Andy Roberts and Michael Holding, two outstanding examples. In addition to Fredericks' 169, Lloyd also went on to a big century, after being dropped by Lillee at mid-on before he scored. The Big Cat hit a ball from yours truly into the swirling, twirling Fremantle Doctor and Lillee ran forward then backwards and ended up on his end having touched the infernal sphere of red leather with his fingertips, but failing to latch on to it. In retrospect attempting to catch that ball was akin to trying to nail a tiddler in a raging surf.

Epilogue

There is something magical about the late spring for it heralds the coming of summer and all the sights and sounds of the greatest game of all. The glorious sound of leather on willow. The aroma of freshly cut grass on an early summer cricket ground. I have always thought the aroma of freshly cut lawn good enough to challenge some of the best aftershave available. (Imagine a bottle of cologne called Freshly Mown flooding the market.)

As a youngster I was fortunate to see the twinkling footwork of Neil Harvey, arguably the best Australian batsman since Don Bradman, dancing yards down the wicket to drive the spinners – and many other great batsmen from England, South Africa and New Zealand. Later, playing at the highest level, I saw firsthand the brilliance of South Africa's Graeme Pollock, Barry Richards, and Mike Procter; England's Ted Dexter, Geoff Boycott (although Boycs' bat usually gave off a somewhat muffled *thwack*), David Gower and Graham Gooch. Playing against the West Indians in the 1970s was some experience. Apart from their barrage of pace bowlers, the Windies had some of the greatest batsman to have drawn breath: Garry Sobers, the greatest all-rounder of them all, Viv Richards, the master-blaster, so too Gordon Greenidge and, of course, the recently knighted, Clive Lloyd.

Although the sound of willow on leather is very much the sound of summer, for a moment on 15 December 1979, with Australia doing battle with England in Perth, the sound of bat on ball was very different when Dennis

Lillee marched to the crease with an aluminium bat. With Ian Botham bowling to Lillee that day, the much-loved *thwack* became a *clunk*. Few liked the idea, especially the England all-rounder. The action of aluminium on leather damaged the ball and, soon enough, the aluminium bat, a temporary aberration, was banned for life.

To me the sound of willow on leather was always the way to go. Fielding close to the wicket I could hear the resounding thud of a Jeff Thomson or Dennis Lillee fireball as it soared into Rodney Marsh's gloves, 30 or so metres behind the stumps. Sometimes he might say, 'Jeez that hurt but I love it!' Always music to the ears of the batsman was the fabulous sound of a sweetly hit ball through the covers, a cut behind point or a savage pull or hook. And the sound of these brilliant strokes always brings a roar from the adoring crowd.

In Sheffield Shield competition, cricket games were once played in a white-hot atmosphere. This was before the international schedule became so congested that the top players rarely turned out for their State sides and almost never for their club team. Bowling to players such as Peter Burge, Brian Booth, Doug Walters, Greg Chappell, Bill Lawry, Kim Hughes, John Inverarity, Ross Edwards and a host of others was always a challenge and a joy. And as a writer I was lucky enough to watch many a big match.

I found great joy in talking at length with such luminaries as Australians Keith Miller, Sir Donald Bradman, Vic Richardson, Bill O'Reilly, Clarrie Grimmett, Bill Brown, Alan Davidson and Neil Harvey, for their stories always enriched my research into the game. Grimmett always spoke passionately about Victor Trumper, the greatest batsman in cricket's Golden Age, and O'Reilly told me about the likes of C.T.B. Turner, the great spinner of the 1880s; even recalling a chance meeting with the famous poet Henry Lawson outside a pub in Milson's Point, Sydney, 20 years before the Sydney Harbour Bridge was completed. Englishmen Frank Woolley, Len Hutton, Tony Lock, Jim Laker, Frank Tyson, Fred Trueman and Denis Compton all helped me fashion stories to bring to you.

The glorious sound of summer begins and ends with a resounding *thwack!* – the moment willow meets leather on the pitch – and will continue to do so for as long as the game of cricket is played.

Acknowledgements

My eternal thanks to the following people whom I either saw in action or played with or against and those of yore whom I didn't see play but researched their lives through many who did so. My aim was always to bring the champions of the past, current and emerging alive in this production.

Sir Gubby Allen*, Jonny Bairstow, David Bairstow*, Alex Barras*, Richie Benaud*, Marcus Bernardi, Billie Birmingham, Sir Donald Bradman*, Lady Jessie Bradman*, Bill Brown*, Ronald Cardwell, Frank Cash*, Mrs Cash*, Rodney Cavalier, Greg Chappell, Jeanne Chappell*, Ian Chappell, Martin Chappell*, Tibby Cotter*, Alexander Crooks*, Alan Davidson, Mike Denness*, Les Favell*, Bill Ferguson*, John Fordham*, Roy Fredericks*, John Gleeson*, W.G. Grace*, Clarrie Grimmett*, Neil Harvey, Vijay Hazare*, Sir Jack Hobbs*, Barry Jarman, Justin Langer, Dennis Lillee, Wally Langdon*, Sir Clive Lloyd, Vinoo Mankad*, Tony Mann*, Grant Mollison, Bill O'Reilly*, Erapally Prasanna, Charlie Puckett*, Ian Redpath, John Rutherford, Sir Vivian Richards, Ken Riches, Fred Riches*, Sir Timothy Rice, Barry Shepherd*, Andrew Stoddart*, Fred Trueman*, Victor Trumper*, Shane Warne, William Alexander Garnaut ('Pop') West*, Mark Nicholas, Bill Whitty*, Frank Woolley*, Dennis Yagmich. (*Deceased)

My thanks to Wakefield Press publisher Michael Bollen for running with this book. Wakefield always produces a quality book. Thanks also to my editor Julia Beaven for her professionalism and expertise.

As I wrote the various stories my mind turned to my family, my brother Nick and my parents, Ray and Clare. They were all very encouraging. And Nick always batted first (every day) in our inevitable backyard 'Tests'. Little wonder I became a specialist bowler.

Special thanks to my wife Patsy whose love and encouragement and first responder look at the copy, sage advice and initial edit continue to be invaluable to me in my writing. During a session of bouncing ideas about a title for this work, Patsy came up with *Thwack! The Glorious Sound of Summer.* Perfect.

Thanks also to Ian Brayshaw, John Inverarity, Trevor Gill, Mark Nicholas and Roger Wills for their general encouragement to me to continue writing.

Wakefield Press is an independent publishing and
distribution company based in Adelaide, South Australia.
We love good stories and publish beautiful books.
To see our full range of books, please visit our website at
www.wakefieldpress.com.au
where all titles are available for purchase.
To keep up with our latest releases, news and events,
subscribe to our monthly newsletter.

Find us!

Facebook: www.facebook.com/wakefield.press
Twitter: www.twitter.com/wakefieldpress
Instagram: www.instagram.com/wakefieldpress

www.ingramcontent.com/pod-product-compliance
Lightning Source LLC
Chambersburg PA
CBHW031357230426
43670CB00006B/569